Blended and Redeemed: The Go-To Field Guide for the Modern Stepfamily Study Guide
Copyright © 2022 by Scott and Vanessa Martindale

This book, or parts thereof, may not be reproduced in any form or by any means without written permission from the publisher, except brief passages for purposes of reviews.

For information, contact XO Marriage™.
P.O Box 59888
Dallas, Texas 75229
1-800-380-6330
xomarriage.com
XO Publishing

Unless otherwise indicated, Scripture quotations are taken from the ESV® Bible (The Holy Bible, English Standard Version®), copyright © 2001 by Crossway, a publishing ministry of Good News Publishers. Used by permission. All rights reserved.

Scripture quotations marked (MSG) are taken from THE MESSAGE, copyright © 1993, 2002, 2018 by Eugene H. Peterson. Used by permission of NavPress, represented by Tyndale House Publishers. All rights reserved.

Scripture quotations taken from the (NASB®) New American Standard Bible®, Copyright © 1960, 1971, 1977, 1995, 2020 by The Lockman Foundation. Used by permission. All rights reserved. www.lockman.org.

Scripture quotations marked (NIV) are taken from the Holy Bible, New International Version®, NIV®. Copyright © 1973, 1978, 1984, 2011 by Biblica, Inc.™ Used by permission of Zondervan. All rights reserved worldwide.
www.zondervan.com. The "NIV" and "New International Version" are trademarks registered in the United States Patent and Trademark Office by Biblica, Inc.™

Any emphasis or parenthetical comments within Scripture are the authors' own.

All rights reserved. No portion of this publication may be reproduced, stored in a retrieval system, or transmitted in any form by any means—electronic, mechanical, photocopying, recording, or any other—without prior permission from the publisher.

ISBN: 978-1-950113-85-9 (Paperback)
ISBN: 978-1-950113-86-6 (eBook)

Printed in the United States of America
22 23 24 25 26—5 4 3 2 1

BLENDED & REDEEMED

STUDY GUIDE

THE GO-TO FIELD GUIDE FOR THE MODERN STEPFAMILY

SCOTT & VANESSA MARTINDALE
Founders of Blended Kingdom Families

CONTENTS

Welcome VII
Leader Guide XI

Chapter 1 Refined in Fire 02
Chapter 2 The Church and Blended Families 12
Chapter 3 Three Priorities for a Healthy Marriage 22
Chapter 4 A Marriage Reflecting God 32
Chapter 5 The False Promise of Inner Vows 44
Chapter 6 Blending Your Bunch 54
Chapter 7 Parenting and Co-Parenting 64
Chapter 8 Facing New Family Challenges Together 76
Chapter 9 Litigation: Your New, Least-Favorite Hobby 88
Chapter 10 Blended Families, God's Redemption 100

Appendix 111
About the Authors 119

WELCOME

Welcome to the *Blended and Redeemed Study Guide*! We (Scott and Vanessa) are so glad you have decided to join us as we take a deep dive into the topic of blended families. The Lord has incredible plans for you, your spouse, and your children, and we are humbled to be a part of your journey.

There are 10 chapters in the *Blended and Redeemed* book, and the same is true for this study guide. Each chapter of this study guide coincides with the chapter of the same number in the book. We highly recommend reading both the book and the study guide in order to gain the most understanding. One of the best aspects of this study guide is that it is designed for individuals, couples, and small groups/classes!

Here is the setup for each chapter, along with some helpful hints and best practices:

1. Key Quote
The key quote is the main takeaway from the chapter.

2. Icebreaker
The icebreaker is a fun or thought-provoking question related to the topic of the chapter.

- *Individuals* may want to journal their responses or share them with their spouse or a friend. You never know how the Holy Spirit might use you to pique someone's interest and help them begin their own journey of growth.
- *Couples* can use this as a way to focus their attention away from the busyness of life and on to the material and each other. Have fun getting to know one another again!
- *Small groups/classes* can be intimidating, and this is a simple

way to help everyone feel more relaxed and comfortable sharing with others.

3. Recap
The recap is a brief summary of the material covered in the previous chapter.

4. Review
The review offers an abbreviated version of the material shared in the corresponding chapter in the *Blended and Redeemed* book.

5. Recommended Scripture Reading
The recommended Scripture reading includes Scriptures to read and meditate on from the chapter.

6. Discussion Questions
The discussion questions are designed as conversation starters for couples and small groups/classes.

- Individuals are welcome to answer these questions too. They may want to record their answers in a journal or share them with their spouse or a friend.

7. Reflection Questions
The reflection questions are geared toward individuals for contemplation and prayer.

- Couples and small groups/classes are welcome to answer these questions too. It is important to note that some questions may be sensitive in nature, and participants may feel more comfortable answering them privately.

8. Assignments
There are two assignments for each chapter:

- Read the next chapter.
- Ask the Lord, "What do You want to teach me?"

No matter how you decide to go through this study guide, we highly recommend using a journal. You will want to write down anything the Lord highlights for you in the material as well as anything He speaks to your heart.

You may be wondering, What is the time commitment for this material? That is an excellent question! If you plan to read it as an individual, then feel free to move at any pace that is comfortable for you. Couples will want to take both spouses' schedules into consideration. You may find that one chapter per week works well, or perhaps one spouse need a little longer. Some seasons might be busier than others, and we want you to know that there is zero pressure. We truly understand that life can be overflowing (in both good and bad ways) at times, and our only desire is for the Lord to bless your marriage and your family in His perfect timing.

The best small groups/classes have clear, consistent expectations. Knowing the time commitment from the outset allows participants to plan and prepare, thus setting them up for success. The following are two sample schedules, one for six weeks and one for ten weeks.

Six-Week Schedule

Week One:	Chapters 1 and 2
Week Two:	Chapters 3 and 4
Week Three:	Chapters 5 and 6
Week Four:	Chapters 7 and 8
Week Five:	Chapters 9 and 10
Week Six:	Celebration

Ten-Week Schedule

Week One:	Chapter 1
Week Two:	Chapter 2
Week Three:	Chapter 3
Week Four:	Chapter 4
Week Five:	Chapter 5
Week Six:	Chapter 6
Week Seven:	Chapter 7
Week Eight:	Chapter 8
Week Nine:	Chapter 9
Week Ten:	Chapter 10 and Celebration

We always recommend ending with a celebration. Your commitment to growing emotionally, mentally, and spiritually as a blended family is no small task, and you deserve to be rewarded! This may look like a special date with your spouse, a fun outing with your family, a party with your small group/class, or something else! Whatever you decide, be sure to take a moment to thank the Lord for everything He has done in your heart. With Him, nothing is impossible!

LEADER GUIDE

We are so grateful you have volunteered to serve as a leader for the *Blended and Redeemed* book study. This may be your first time leading a book study, or you may have a great deal of experience. Either way, we believe the Holy Spirit will guide and use you to bless the couples in your small group/class as He speaks to their hearts and strengthens their families. We also believe you will be blessed as well!

The following are guidelines to leading a book study. We offer a sample session schedule to help you structure your sessions and cover the material in an organized fashion. We also include some practical advice on preparing for and leading the sessions. You may find that some things work wonderfully for your small group/class while other aspects need adjustment. That is perfectly fine! The most important thing for you to do as a leader is to pray and hear the Holy Spirit's desire and direction. His plan is always the best plan!

SAMPLE SESSION SCHEDULE
1. Welcome and Icebreaker: 5 minutes
2. Recap: 5 minutes
3. Read: 20 minutes
4. Discussion: 20 minutes
5. Prayer: 10 minutes

For the first session, use the Recap time to help the couples get to know each other. Invite each couple to share the following information with the small group/class:

1. Names
2. How long they've been married
3. How many children they have

For the remaining sessions, use the Recap time to summarize the previous session's chapter.

PREPARING FOR THE SESSIONS

1. Pray

The best way to begin preparing for each session is to ask the Lord for His guidance. He knows the needs, desires, and hopes of each person in your small group/class, as well as what you need to be an impactful leader. What should you pray about? Here are a few ideas:

- Pray for each person's relationship with the Lord.
- Pray for each person's relationship with their spouse.
- Pray for each couple's relationship with their children.
- Pray for the Holy Spirit to give you wisdom and to speak through you.

Don't be afraid to ask God to do big things! He is a great God who can move mountains and separate seas, and there is nothing too hard for Him.

2. Plan

Read the chapter in both the book and the study guide that you will be discussing in the next session. (For example, before the first session, read Chapter 1 in *Blended and Redeemed* and in this study guide.) Make notes about anything that stands out to you, such as quotes, Scriptures, stories, etc. Next, review the discussion questions. Choose two that you believe will garner the greatest interest and foster conversation. If time permits during the session, you can also ask the remaining discussion questions.

Ask someone to be a backup leader in the event that an emergency prevents you from attending a session. This may be your spouse, your pastor, a mature small group/class member, or someone else whom you trust to guide the book study.

3. Pray (Again!)

As you wrap up your planning, it is time to pray again. Why? Well, first of all, there is no such thing as "too much" prayer. We need the Holy Spirit's help every moment! Second, this prayer is one of submission. Submit all your plans to the Lord. He has a special purpose for this book study, and while it is important to be prepared, it's even more important to be flexible. Allow each session to be led by the Holy Spirit. Remember, a godly leader facilitates, not dictates.

LEADING THE SESSIONS

1. Be Punctual

Nothing says "I don't care" like a leader who is habitually late. Are we saying tardiness is the unforgiveable leadership sin? Not at all. Life comes with surprises and situations that can get in the way of our good intentions. Still, do your best to be on time—or better yet, early—to every session. In the event that you may be late or even absent for a session, have a backup leader prepared. Beginning (and ending) promptly will show the couples in your small group/class that you honor their time.

2. Be Engaged

The couples in your small group/class will mirror your level of engagement. The more engaged you are, the more engaged they will be too! *Be fully present*. Do everything you can to eliminate distractions. This may require you to turn off your cell phone for the hour or put it on "silent"/"do not disturb" mode.

During the discussion time in the first session, set the example of being open and vulnerable (using godly discretion, of course) and let the couples know that everything shared in the sessions will stay within the small group/class. Creating a safe space will foster greater engagement as couples become more comfortable. Being engaged doesn't mean you have to have the "perfect" answers or be the person who talks the most. In fact, it is better to allow some moments of "awkward" silence as the couples think through the questions themselves.

3. Be Compassionate

To make a major understatement, blended families have been through a lot. And whether they choose to share the details, the couples in your small group/class will probably still be going through a lot. There may be times when someone acts disengaged and withdrawn, or they may be highly emotional and domineering of the conversation. These are the perfect moments to demonstrate the heart of our heavenly Father. Psalm 86:15 says, "You, Lord, are a compassionate and gracious God, slow to anger, abounding in love and faithfulness" (NIV). Allow the Holy Spirit to guide your words, actions, and demeanor. He will give you wisdom in how you relate to each person in your small group/class. And don't forget to be compassionate toward yourself. There will probably be moments when you feel under-qualified or ill-prepared. Just remember that there is only one perfect Leader, and He is the King of kings and Lord of lords. Keep your eyes on Jesus because "he's the one who will keep you on track" (Proverbs 3:6 MSG).

CHAPTER 1

REFINED IN FIRE

"Like Shadrach, Meshach, and Abednego, we were sitting among the flames, but God was with us in the furnace."

ICEBREAKER
Describe something God asked you to do that surprised you.

REVIEW
Our family, the Martindale family, is a blended Kingdom family. We (Scott and Vanessa) both come from blended families, and now we have one of our own. Our blend—just like yours—is made up of different people, different backgrounds, and different personalities all mixed together to form one family. We each bring something beautiful and unique, and we each bring our mess and old baggage. And we have the the sometimes-impossible task of figuring out how to make all these pieces fit together.

The year 2017 was supposed to be a year we could catch our breath, but it became 12 long months of all-out spiritual warfare and attacks from Satan, whom we call the "enemy." Chances are, you have walked through seasons such as ours—times of complete desperation and opposition in which you found yourself on your knees in full submission to God. In those moments of hopelessness, we discovered that kneeling before the Father was the safest place we could be. When we knelt before Him, the refining process began. We laid down our pride, surrendered everything to God, and died to our flesh every single day in our prayer closet. Like He did for Shadrach, Meshach, and Abednego, God walked us through fire, and we emerged from the flames completely changed, refined, and victorious.

We are all blended in the Kingdom of God. The apostle John writes

> After this I looked, and behold, a great multitude that no one could number, from every nation, from all tribes and peoples and languages, standing before the throne and before the Lamb, clothed in white robes, with palm branches in their hands (Revelation 7:9).

What a beautiful picture of the family of God. Our identity is not in the *blend* (or as some people call it, the *stepfamily*) but as heirs in the Kingdom.

A traditional family might be compared to a piece of fine jewelry. It's meticulously crafted out of the finest, unblemished materials and turned into a single piece, an original work of art. But what happens when that family falls apart? The jewelry shatters, and the father, mother, and children each walk away with their own tiny pieces. They bring those shards with them into their new relationships and ultimately into their new families. But how is a new family supposed to merge into something new and beautiful when all the old pieces won't fit together? They have to be refined—*refined by fire*. For the good of the family we're crafting, we must trust these precious pieces to God, the Master Craftsman and Ultimate Refiner.

The heart of Blended Kingdom Families (BKF) is reflected in Isaiah 61:1–3:

> He has sent me to bind up the brokenhearted, to proclaim freedom for the captives
> and release from darkness for the prisoners ...
> to comfort all who mourn,
> and provide for those who grieve in Zion—
> *to bestow on them a crown of beauty*

instead of ashes,
the oil of joy
instead of mourning,
and a garment of praise
instead of a spirit of despair (NIV, emphasis added).

God wants to turn your old, broken, and tarnished pieces into a "crown of beauty." He wants to take your mourning and give you joy and replace your despair with pure praise. He can, and He will. But it's not easy. Tossing those pieces of our old life into the fire and watching them melt away is hard—sometimes harder than we think we can bear. This is something our family knows all too well, but we are also deeply acquainted with and in awe of the beauty the Father offers us on the other side of the fire. We've seen the crown of beauty He had in store for our family, and we can encourage you by our experience that it was worth the journey.

Starting in the spring of 2017, we (Scott and Vanessa) found ourselves in the toughest spiritual battle we had ever faced. It was physically, mentally, and emotionally exhausting all day, every day. We didn't realize it at first, but we were heading straight into the fire that would ultimately refine our hearts, minds, and every aspect of our blended family.

I (Vanessa) soon found myself succumbing to the enemy's lies: that there was no hope for victory, and defeat would soon be my portion. I cried out to God morning and night. Then, one night, God answered with a vivid dream. I was wearing a ragged wedding dress, and a woman showed me a journal with my new name—*Redeemed*. She explained that a new, perfect wedding gown had been prepared for me. I could see it from a distance, but the gown remained just out of reach. Then I woke up.

The next day, a close friend shared that the Lord had led her to a passage of Scripture from the book of Daniel and given her a word of encouragement to pass along to me. The passage began with the morning after Shadrach, Meshach and Abednego had been condemned to spend the night in a fiery furnace because of their faithfulness to God:

> Nebuchadnezzar then approached the opening of the blazing furnace and shouted, "Shadrach, Meshach and Abednego, servants of the Most High God, come out! Come here!"
>
> So Shadrach, Meshach and Abednego came out of the fire, and the satraps, prefects, governors and royal advisers crowded around them. They saw that the fire had not harmed their bodies, nor was a hair of their heads singed; their robes were not scorched, and there was no smell of fire on them (Daniel 3:26–27 NIV).

As my friend read that passage over me, it felt as if God, in His infinite goodness, had divinely smacked me over the head with a spiritual two-by-four as He revealed the meaning of my dream. We were in the fire! Like Shadrach, Meshach, and Abednego, we were sitting among the flames, but God was with us in the furnace. I realized that I hadn't been touched by the flames. I didn't even smell like smoke. I had simply emerged tired and worn.

God reminded me that like Shadrach, Meshach, and Abednego, He never promised to keep us out of the fire. He only promised to walk through it with us. God made it clear that His plans were to prosper us and to use this agonizing situation for our good and His glory.

Following that season of refinement, we had a time of rest. I (Vanessa) felt God reveal that this rest was intended to prepare and equip us for an important work in the upcoming season.

God said the very thing many believe disqualifies us for service in His Kingdom is the very thing He would use to qualify us. He asked, "Would you help Me build Blended Kingdom Families?"

I knew this was a call into full-time ministry. God wanted to use our family to strengthen, equip, and encourage other families who were facing the same kinds of struggles and obstacles we had experienced. Everything had led to this moment, in which the Lord exchanged our tears and trials for a revelation that everything we'd endured was for His greater glory and ultimate purpose.

When we officially launched the BKF ministry in January 2020, we had three immediate goals:

1. Develop a class, curriculum, and book to be used in church groups to strengthen and equip blended families across the ministry spectrum, from marriage to parenting to children's struggles.
2. Immediately offer resources to families by launching an audio and video podcast in which we could not only share our story and the stories of other blended families, but also conduct in-depth interviews with pastors, counselors, and family ministry experts on topics specifically geared toward marriage and blended families.
3. Create the Blended Kingdom Project in which we would dedicate days, nights, and weekends to gleaning information from blended couples to better understand who they were, where they were coming from, and what they were dealing with.

The Blended Kingdom Project consists of two key components: a survey and a face-to-face interview. We've been conducting the project a couple of years now, and we've interviewed more than 60 families to date from all over the world. Remembering the Great Commission to make disciples of all nations (Matthew 28:19), we wanted to cast a wide net to gain a solid understanding of the needs of blended families locally, nationally, and globally.

As believers, we have a very real enemy—Satan—who wants to devour our marriages, steal our children, and destroy our lives. The institution of family holds tremendous influence over individuals and society as a whole. Satan hates that, and he has tried to interfere with marriages since God formed Adam and Eve in the Garden of Eden. We (Scott and Vanessa) learned to see the devil's schemes during the worst time in our life. He almost ran off with our family, but God broke through and saved us. God will do the same for you too!

Our mission is to come alongside you and see blended families become blended Kingdom families. We believe God is calling our ministry to become a powerful force for the Kingdom by breaking the generational cycle of divorce and bringing revival to the Church. The enemy knows a family that's unified and fortified by the blood of Christ is one of God's most powerful weapons in advancing His Kingdom on earth. Our prayer for the book and this study guide is that they will equip your marriage and blended family and help you draw closer to God, your spouse, and your children. We pray you will be healed and find forgiveness for yourself and for anyone who has hurt you in the past. We understand the unique difficulties you and your family face, and we hope that through Blended Kingdom Families, you will find community, support, and encouragement.

RECOMMEND SCRIPTURE READING

Nebuchadnezzar then approached the opening of the blazing furnace and shouted, "Shadrach, Meshach and Abednego, servants of the Most High God, come out! Come here!"

So Shadrach, Meshach and Abednego came out of the fire, and the satraps, prefects, governors and royal advisers crowded around them. They saw that the fire had not harmed their bodies, nor was a hair of their heads singed; their robes were not scorched, and there was no smell of fire on them (Daniel 3:26–27 NIV).

He has sent me to bind up the brokenhearted,
to proclaim freedom for the captives
and release from darkness for the prisoners ...
to comfort all who mourn,
and provide for those who grieve in Zion—
to bestow on them a crown of beauty
instead of ashes,
the oil of joy
instead of mourning,
and a garment of praise
instead of a spirit of despair (Isaiah 61:1–3 NIV, emphasis added).

But thanks be to God! He gives us the victory through our Lord Jesus Christ (1 Corinthians 15:57).

Be alert and of sober mind. Your enemy the devil prowls around like a roaring lion looking for someone to devour (1 Peter 5:8 NIV).

The thief comes only to steal and kill and destroy; I have come that they may have life, and have it to the full (John 10:10 NIV).

DISCUSSION QUESTIONS

1. What is one thing you wish traditional families understood about blended families?

_____

_____

_____

_____

2. How does it make you feel to know that as believers, we are all part of the blended Kingdom of God?

3. How would you encourage someone who is going through a "fire" season right now?

4. Read Daniel 3:16–27. What does this passage tell you about God when His people are in the fire?

REFLECTION QUESTIONS

1. In what ways is the enemy coming against your family? How can you stand against him?

2. God spoke to Vanessa in a dream. What are some ways He speaks to you?

___

3. What vision, mission, or purpose has God placed on your heart? (This could be for yourself, your family, or the body of Christ.)

___

PRAYER

Father God, thank You for always being with us. Refining seasons can feel so difficult, but You promise in Your Word that You will never leave us or forsake us. Your presence is the safest place we can be. We choose today to trust You. Please open our ears to hear Your voice and open our eyes to see how You are working in our lives. Thank You for allowing us to be a part of Your blended Kingdom family. In Jesus' name, Amen.

ASSIGNMENT
- Read Chapter 2 in *Blended and Redeemed*.
- Ask the Lord, "What do You want to teach me?"

CHAPTER 2

THE CHURCH AND BLENDED FAMILIES

"By providing resources and simple acknowledgment, churches can help normalize the existence of the blended families in their congregations."

ICEBREAKER

If you could write an instruction manual on blended families, what would be the title?

RECAP

Refining seasons can feel endlessly and utterly difficult, but they serve a purpose: they prepare us for God's incredible plans and purposes for our lives. God wants to take our broken pieces and turn them into a "crown of beauty" (see Isaiah 61:1–3). He never promised to keep us out of the fire, but He does promise to walk through it with us. His plans are to prosper us and to use our situations for our good and His glory.

God asked us (Scott and Vanessa) to build Blended Kingdom Families (BKF) to strengthen, encourage, and equip other families who are facing the same difficulties we've experienced. Satan is a real enemy who wants to destroy our families, but we can fight back through the power of prayer and the truth of God's Word. A family that's unified and fortified by the blood of Christ is one of God's most powerful weapons in advancing His Kingdom on earth.

REVIEW

Most churches have a full schedule of small groups, Bible studies, conferences, camps, workshops, and discipleship programs for all age groups. However, it's rare to find something specifically designed for blended families. Blended families have unique needs and struggles—things their well-meaning, "traditional family" friends have difficulty understanding. Most blended families sitting in church on Sunday morning feel like they are alone. Some are scared, others are confused, and most are hurting. They may be dealing with child behavioral issues, custody battles, co-parenting difficulties, old wounds affecting their new marriage, guilt, shame, fear, or isolation. Whom are they talking to about it? Whom are they connecting with? Sadly, the answer is probably no one.

Based on our experience in working with blended families and conducting the Blended Kingdom Project, there are two main reasons for this:

1. It seems more difficult for blended families to find people who understand what they're going through and who can relate to their situation. They wish there were more resources and opportunities to meet other families on a similar journey, especially inside the church.
2. Blended families feel a lot of ambiguity about their place in the church, and the majority carry the weight of shame because of their situation. Many will walk into church on Sunday morning, force a smile as they engage with others, and bury their hurt until they get back home.

All this may sound sad and depressing, but it represents one of the greatest untapped ministry opportunities of all time!

If the church can tap into this enormous need, it can bring hope to countless families *immediately*. It can save couples from experiencing a second or third divorce. It would give the church the opportunity to turn back decades of increasing divorce rate statistics by divorce-proofing the next generation. Most of all, the church could make the gospel relevant to hurting families who are already sitting in the pews while also expanding the Kingdom by bringing in hurting families who aren't. We are reminded of the repeated theme of Jesus' compassion throughout the Gospel of Matthew:

> When he saw the crowds, he had compassion for them, because they were harassed and helpless, like sheep without a shepherd. Then he said to his disciples, "The harvest is plentiful, but the laborers are few; therefore, pray earnestly to the Lord of the harvest to send out laborers into his harvest" (Matthew 9:36–38).

As disciples, leaders, ministers, pastors, and mentors, we are admonished in Scripture to show compassion to those in need—including blended families. Our prayer is that more and more "laborers" would approach this much-needed ministry and bring forth compassion-filled opportunities for their marriages and families. Blended families are looking for someone to come alongside them, shepherd them, and help them through their journey.

If you happen to be in a church that is equipping your blended marriage and family, we are celebrating with you. We love it when we see or hear of churches supporting stepfamilies. On the other hand, I (Scott) didn't know a single blended family in the church I grew up in, and divorce and remarriage were never mentioned from the pulpit. That type of silence around the topic can leave churchgoers feeling like their family isn't accepted in the church and that they don't have a place there.

When all a hurting family hears is silence, two assumptions are made:

1. No one cares about our need.
2. This is a private problem we need to solve on our own.

That explains why people who find our Blended Kingdom Families ministry get so excited by all the BKF podcasts, videos, articles, classes, and curriculum. People are shocked to discover that someone—*anyone*—is taking this need seriously enough to fill up YouTube with videos, interviews, and teachings specifically on remarriage and stepparenting.

Let's not lose sight of the fact that children in blended families need help as well! Imagine a child going to children's ministry or youth activities at their church every single week and never hearing a word about the issues that are troubling them the most. They hear about drinking, sex, drugs, bullying, peer pressure, and even getting along with their parents, but nobody ever talks about what to do when your parents get divorced or you suddenly get a new mom or dad. These are the most life-changing events of these children's lives, and they are often left to sort it out with little or no help.

Blended families happen in a variety of ways, including one or both spouses having gone through a divorce, the death of a spouse, or one or both spouses having a child out of wedlock at some point in the past. Sadly, divorce and sex outside of marriage are two topics some pastors and churches struggle to talk about with grace and truth. *Grace* and *truth* are the key words here because these are difficult, complicated topics that are completely drenched in raw emotion.

When churches do talk about divorce, it sometimes comes across as only a dire warning to protect your marriage from divorce at all costs. While that's great advice, it doesn't speak to the people who have already been through a divorce. And if divorce is only ever associated with sin and failure, then the people who have gone through it or are going through it tend to keep their mouths shut. What's missing is a biblical understanding of divorce and the implications it has on remarriage, stepfamilies, and the church's role in these families' lives.

When Christians don't get solid, biblical instruction on the topics of divorce, divorce recovery, and remarriage, a great deal of *inferred judgment* works its way through congregations. Many churchgoers may get a sense that the Bible makes no allowance for divorce whatsoever, that it's always a sin, and that it's something "civilized Christians just don't talk about." That quiet dismissal leaves anyone who has been through a divorce stuck outside the gates of community.

Divorce is not "the unforgiveable sin." While divorce is the result of someone's sin, God can, will, and does forgive us when we repent, and His forgiveness is absolute. The sin is gone "as far as the east is from the west" (Psalm 103:12). Romans 8:1 tells us, "There is therefore now *no condemnation* for those who are in Christ Jesus" (emphasis added). Of course, that doesn't mean a divorce borne of sin is no big deal. It is a huge deal, both to God and to the heartbroken people involved. But where there is repentance, there is also forgiveness and the unending grace of our Father.

What about the victims of divorce? We believe there is biblical support for a handful of situations in which the victim of divorce is 100 percent free of the marriage:

1. Adultery (Matthew 19:9)
2. Abuse (1 Corinthians 7:15–16)
3. Abandonment (Matthew 18:15–17; 1 Corinthians 7:15–16)
4. Addiction (1 Corinthians 7:15–16)

Even if you were the adulterer, abuser, abandoner, or addict, God can and will still forgive you of that sin when you come to Him in repentance. And if He forgives you for your actions in the divorce, He can certainly bless your new marriage.

As followers of Christ who are striving to bring glory to God and expand His Kingdom on earth, we can't knowingly ignore half the families in our community—or drive out half the families in our congregations—simply because we can't get our arms around God's view of divorce, remarriage, and forgiveness. The cost is too great.

We've never had *fewer* people in church and *more* people in blended families than we do right now. If the church rose up as the place for blended families to receive support, encouragement, and community, we could strengthen families and reduce the chances of more divorces while at the same time growing the church and the Kingdom. This could be the single greatest opportunity for discipleship and growth in our lifetime!

The first step toward creating a safe environment where blended family members can experience God in a new way is to make your church a no-shame and no-guilt zone regarding divorce and remarriage. Temper truth with grace. Even in the worst circumstances, divorce, sex outside of marriage, and having a child out of wedlock are all forgivable. The Bible makes it clear that God can and will forgive those who come to Him in repentance. If God forgives, who are we to keep that family's sin alive?

The second step is to offer resources *for* blended families *about* blended families. The church should not only focus on the deep, spiritual needs of its members, but it should also offer practical, faith-based resources to help improve their everyday lives. By resources, we mean things like a class, book, workbook, group study, video curriculum, small group, workshop, seminar, conference—literally anything that specifically addresses the needs of blended families. By providing resources and simple acknowledgment, churches can help normalize the existence of the blended families in their congregations.

Finally, the most powerful thing the church can do to support blended families might just be the easiest thing: help blended families connect with each other. Newly blended families often feel out of place in traditional family ministry groups and classes because they have unique needs. They require a community that understands what they're going through. This could be as simple as offering Sunday School class and/or small group options specifically for couples who have remarried and have stepchildren. Blended families need to see where and how they belong. Your church can go a long way toward ministering to them by making it obvious.

If blended families have been traditionally underserved in

your church, now is the time to step things up a notch. The upside is enormous:

- We get to see the Kingdom of God advance through marriage and family in a new way.
- It's an opportunity to strengthen second and third marriages (remarriages) that might otherwise continue the cycle of divorce.
- It's a chance to wrap our children in the armor of God—both spiritually and practically—to protect them from the pitfalls and schemes of the enemy during difficult times.
- It's a generational game-changer that prepares children for the hard work of their own future marriages, thereby changing future generations and building a legacy of strong families.

Most importantly, it's an opportunity for more people to come to know Jesus. By meeting this need, the church positions itself as a loving, helpful resource during the worst time in someone's life, bringing hope to those already in the congregation, and attracting those outside who are looking for help.

RECOMMENDED SCRIPTURE READING

When he saw the crowds, he had compassion for them, because they were harassed and helpless, like sheep without a shepherd. Then he said to his disciples, "The harvest is plentiful, but the laborers are few; therefore pray earnestly to the Lord of the harvest to send out laborers into his harvest" (Matthew 9:36–38).

If we confess our sins, he is faithful and just to forgive us our sins and to cleanse us from all unrighteousness (1 John 1:9).

As far as the east is from the west, so far does he remove our transgressions from us (Psalm 103:12).

There is therefore now no condemnation for those who are in Christ Jesus (Romans 8:1).

DISCUSSION QUESTIONS

1. How does your church respond to blended families?

2. What sermons or teachings have you heard about divorce, remarriage, and blended families?

3. Why do you think Christians sometimes struggle to find a balance between grace and truth?

4. How can you encourage pastors and other leaders to make a safe, welcoming space for blended families within the local church?

REFLECTION QUESTIONS

1. What resources have been the most helpful as you've transitioned into blended family life?

2. What additional resources have you needed or wished existed but been unable to find?

3. In a "perfect" world, how would the local church respond to your blended family?

PRAYER

Father God, You designed the church to be an earthly expression of Your perfect love. Please forgive us for the times we have failed to make people—Your most precious creation—feel welcome and safe. Thank You for Your mercy that is new every morning. We receive Your grace today. May our lives be a constant reflection of Your kindness and compassion. In Jesus' name, Amen.

ASSIGNMENT

- Read Chapter 3 in *Blended and Redeemed*.
- Ask the Lord, "What do You want to teach me?"

CHAPTER 3

THREE PRIORITIES FOR A HEALTHY MARRIAGE

"Strong marriages make strong children, and godly marriages make Kingdom families."

ICEBREAKER
What is your favorite activity to do as a family?

RECAP
Blended families have unique needs and struggles, and most blended families sitting in church on Sunday morning feel like they are alone. They wish there were more resources and opportunities to meet other families on a similar journey, and they feel a lot of ambiguity about their place in the body of Christ.

Divorce is not "the unforgiveable sin." Whether you were the perpetrator or victim of divorce, there is forgiveness and unending grace from our heavenly Father. He even wants to bless your new marriage! Churches must learn to preach both truth and grace and provide a safe, shame-free environment where blended families can experience the love of God. If the local church rose up as the place for blended families to receive support, encouragement, and community, we could strengthen families, reduce the chances of more divorces, and expand the Kingdom of God.

REVIEW
One of the biggest problems in a remarriage is unclear or misaligned priorities, and the biggest offender is prioritizing your children above the marriage. This is an especially big problem if

the children have been in a single-parent home for a while. They get used to having Mom or Dad all to themselves. When a new spouse is added to the mix, jealousy can run wild. The parent, then, can react out of guilt and overcompensate by giving the children the number-one spot in his or her life. The problem, of course, is that this leaves no room for the new spouse. This issue is magnified exponentially if *both* spouses bring kids into the new marriage and struggle to keep their priorities in check.

Doing marriage God's way means setting your priorities early and defending them often. The top three priorities are:

1. Your relationship with Christ
2. Your marriage
3. Your children

By aligning your marriage God's way, you'll empower yourself to deal with past pain, lay a strong foundation for your relationship, and prepare yourself for the challenges of blended family life.

Our top priority is our relationship with Jesus. The Bible says, "Seek *first* the kingdom of God and his righteousness, and all these things will be added to you" (Matthew 6:33, emphasis added). We must make Christ the head of our life, marriage, and family as we seek to honor and glorify Him in everything we do. When we get married, we make a covenant with God. Yes, your spouse is a part of this, but you are making your vow unto the Lord. Therefore, when you seek Him and His Kingdom first, everything else will be given to you in your life, marriage, and blended family.

Picture it like a triangle. The point at the top represents Jesus, and the two points at the bottom represent you and your spouse respectively. The closer each of you grows toward God, the closer you're going to grow in your relationship with one another. But if one or both of you puts anything else at the top of the triangle, Christ gets pushed down or off to the side. Your priorities then come out of alignment with His, which can throw off your spiritual walk, and that throws your marriage off.

Faith isn't reserved for Sunday mornings and Wednesday nights only; we should engage in our relationship with the Lord every day, throughout the day. It's a daily practice and discipline, a consistent and persistent relationship with the One who knows us inside and out and loves us through and through. The problem for so many couples is that our schedules usually don't offer us "free time" to spend with the Lord, which is ironic considering He is the Author of time. He created it so we could spend our days and hours with Him, not distant from Him. When God isn't our top priority, He'll only get our leftovers. But God doesn't want our leftovers, nor does He deserve the lack of attention. He wants our *best*, and He wants it *first*. And He deserves every bit of it.

The amazing thing is that when we make God the top priority in our life, it doesn't mean we're left with less to give everyone and everything else. Instead, it leaves us with more. In John 15:5, Jesus says, "I am the vine; you are the branches. If you remain in me and I in you, *you will bear much fruit*; apart from me you can do nothing" (NIV, emphasis added). What can we do apart from Him? *Nothing*. What can we do when we remain in Him? We can and will bear much fruit. We'll have more to share with our spouse, children, friends, work, and everything else in our lives.

If your current spiritual life feels more like you're talking at God rather than talking *with* God, we recommend adding three simple daily habits to your routine:

1. Start reading one chapter a day in the Bible.
2. Set aside intentional time for prayer.
3. Devote 10–15 minutes a day in quiet time—alone with no distractions.

Your greatest responsibility as a parent is to raise up children who love the Lord more than anything else. You can only do that when *you* love the Lord more than anything else.

According to Scripture, the thing you should love most in this world—a close second to your love for Christ—is the love you feel for your spouse. That love will be reflected in how much time and attention—in other words, how much *priority*—you give him or her. That's how God designed marriage from the beginning. Genesis 2:24 says a husband will *"hold fast* to his wife, and they shall become *one flesh"* (emphasis added). That's how close a husband and wife should be: so close that they're considered one flesh. Putting anything—even your children—between you and your spouse will cheat you of the blessings God wants to pour into your marriage.

Your love for your spouse will be demonstrated through your intimacy and time. Physical intimacy isn't the only form of intimacy, although sex is definitely important. Intimacy is also spiritual (praying and worshipping together), emotional (talking and connecting together), and financial (stewarding your God-given resources together). Remember, one flesh means becoming one in *all* aspects of your life and marriage.

God doesn't want your leftover time, and neither does your spouse. Many couples build their marriages around everything *except* God and each other. They let life drag them around by the nose instead of planting a flag and claiming time for themselves as husband and wife. If you aren't intentional about making time for your marriage, you'll almost certainly experience a gradual decline in marital satisfaction until you bottom out and either divorce or settle in for the lonely and loveless long haul. It was never God's intention for you to survive through your marriage. No, He wants you to thrive in it! Jesus tells us in the Gospel of John, "The thief comes only to steal and kill and destroy. I came so that they may have life and have it abundantly" (John 10:10).

One way to be on the same page with your spouse is to schedule daily and weekly touchpoints to communicate. Touchpoints are kid-free times to have mental, physical, emotional, or spiritual intimacy with your spouse. A daily check-in is a block of time (usually 15 minutes to one hour) set aside to discuss the events of the day, review urgent issues, talk about FYIs, and even spend intimate time together. Make time to go before the Lord together as a couple every day. It doesn't have to be long or complicated—God hears simple prayers too!

Marriage is *not* the end of your dating life. In fact, it's the beginning of a God-honoring service to your spouse and marriage. Whether you've been married for 10 weeks or 10 years, you should pursue your spouse with the same intensity you had when you were dating.

Every couple needs to date. It could be going out to dinner and a movie, seeing a show together, playing cards or games on a double date with another couple ... Whatever you did while you were falling in love, keep doing it! Your yearly calendar should be full of weekly date nights and regular one-on-one getaways like weekend trips, marriage retreats, and anniversary vacations. Show your spouse they matter by carving out time just for them. No work, no cell phones, no soccer games, and *no kids*! Date night is not family night. It's a special night to be cherished and protected with your spouse.

Date nights are for fun and intimacy, so try to avoid any "heavy" conversations about big issues or anything involving the calendar when you're on a date. For those things, we recommend scheduling a weekly Marriage and Family Business Meeting. This is a regular, scheduled meeting in which the two heads of the family—the husband and wife—meet to discuss two key areas: marriage (vision and direction for your relationship) and family business (social commitments, work engagements, vacation plans, etc.). If possible, give this meeting a permanent spot on your calendar with the same day, time, and location each week. As with the other touchpoints, there is a strict "no kids allowed" policy for this meeting. This is the time for Mom and Dad to handle the "business" of the family.

Parents don't go into a second or third marriage planning for it to fail. They're hoping for the best while trying to provide the safest environment for their children However, many parents misunderstand what *safe* means to a child. Children thrive in environments of structure and stability, and the safest, most stable place a child can be is in a home with two parents who put each other first in every circumstance. Strong marriages make strong children, and godly marriages make Kingdom families.

When children have structure and routine and know what's coming, they experience less stress and anxiety. Blended kids have to keep up with two different family routines, and those systems are often as different as night and day. Just when they get settled into one routine, they have to go to the other house to fall into *that* routine. Many families report that the child who comes and goes usually needs a day or two (or ten) to adjust to the different dynamic. Our hearts are deeply burdened for these children, and we have felt that very anxiety and dysfunction ourselves. We know it's hard to grow strong roots if you're constantly being uprooted.

Even though children are the third priority in this list, they should never feel like they're in third place. You can prioritize your time with God and your spouse without cheating your kids by following two simple rules. **First, make weekends and evenings with the kids sacred.** If you work traditional daytime hours at your job, then strive to dedicate your nights and weekends to your family. That means letting calls go to voicemail, not checking email, and not racing to the phone to check every text that comes through. Of course, there will be exceptions—life happens. No matter how much you guard your schedule, you'll have to jump in and help save the day from time to time. Just make sure these things *stay* exceptions.

Time with our families is precious and valuable, and it's not something we can buy more of. When your kids are little or when you're early in the blending process, structure will come from consistent routines, family rules, and setting boundaries. We recommend setting a regular dinnertime and eating at the table together to discuss everyone's day. Our research showed that satisfaction levels and family unity were lower for those families who did not participate in a daily family meal together.

Second, say no to things. Nothing gives you more time in your day than simply saying no. Your top three priorities are Christ, your spouse, and your children, so everything else in your life must be prioritized around the big three. Just because something is *good* doesn't mean it is a *priority* or a God-thing. If something takes you away from your top priorities or leaves you too tired or too busy to engage in your relationships with Christ, your spouse, and your kids, then it's a *no*. To make it easier on yourself, try asking God what He wants you to do in those "opportunity moments." He will be sure to tell you to either pick it up or lay it down.

The greatest gift you can give your child is a godly, happy, healthy, and structured home life, and the core of your family is your marriage. Everything you do to improve your marriage will, in turn, strengthen your children. Our goal as parents, then, should be to demonstrate a godly marriage for our kids—and this doesn't apply only to *your* marriage. If your ex is also remarried, you should do whatever you can to support them in their marriage, too. How great would it be if your child was surrounded by two fully functional, loving homes with strong marriages that glorified God? Come on now—that's revival in the family!

RECOMMEND SCRIPTURE READING

Wives, submit to your own husbands, as to the Lord.... Now as the church submits to Christ, so also wives should submit in everything to their husbands.

Husbands, love your wives, as Christ loved the church and gave himself up for her.... In the same way husbands should love their wives as their own bodies. He who loves his wife loves himself (Ephesians 5:22, 24–25, 28).

Seek *first* the kingdom of God and his righteousness, and all these things will be added to you (Matthew 6:33, emphasis added).

I am the vine; you are the branches. If you remain in me and I in you, *you will bear much fruit*; apart from me you can do *nothing* (John 15:5 NIV, emphasis added).

Rejoice always, pray without ceasing, give thanks in all circumstances; for this is the will of God in Christ Jesus for you (1 Thessalonians 5:16–18).

The thief comes only to steal and kill and destroy. I came so that they may have life and have it abundantly (John 10:10).

Look carefully then how you walk, not as unwise but wise, *making the best use of the time* (Ephesians 5:15–16, emphasis added.)

DISCUSSION QUESTIONS

1. What are the world's top priorities in a family? How do these differ from God's priorities?

2. Why do you think some parents prioritize their children above everything else?

3. How will strengthening your marriage strengthen your children?

4. Why is it important to know the difference between a good thing and a God-thing?

___

REFLECTION QUESTIONS

1. If you were to list your priorities based on how you are currently spending your time, what would they be?

___

2. How would daily and weekly touchpoints impact your marriage?

___

3. How should you respond if an ex-spouse tries to use your godly priorities against you?

___

PRAYER

Father God, we want to do marriage Your way. Please help us establish our priorities in the correct order as we seek Your Kingdom above everything else. Teach us to say yes to the things that will honor You and bless our marriage and children. Give us wisdom and courage to say no to everything else. Whenever we get distracted or discouraged, we believe that You will graciously guide us back to the right path. We love You, Lord, and we pray that You will be glorified in our lives. In Jesus' name, Amen.

ASSIGNMENT
- Read Chapter 4 in *Blended and Redeemed*.
- Ask the Lord, "What do You want to teach me?"

CHAPTER 4

A MARRIAGE REFLECTING GOD

"A marriage that reflects God is a marriage that reflects God's grace."

ICEBREAKER
Where did you go for your honeymoon? Where would you like to go in the future?

RECAP
Doing marriage God's way means setting your priorities early and defending them often. Your first priority is your relationship with Christ. When you seek the Lord and His Kingdom first, everything else will be given to you in your life, marriage, and blended family.

Your relationship with your spouse is your second priority. Being "one flesh" means becoming one in *all* aspects of your life and marriage—physically, spiritually, emotionally, and financially. Pray together, go on dates, and make time to communicate and connect through daily and weekly touchpoints.

Your relationship with your children is your third priority. Make weekends and evenings with the kids sacred, guarding your schedule from interruptions. Learn to say "no" to anything that takes you away from your top priorities or leaves you too tired or too busy to engage in your relationships with Christ, your spouse, and your kids.

REVIEW
According to Scripture, God not only made men and women, but

He also made them to be together. And He blessed them! If our eyes are fixed on Christ first, then our marriages will be overflowing with joy and blessings. We've heard so many amazing stories from other blended family marriages who participated in the BKF Project. They've told us that when they established Jesus Christ as the center and focal point of their marriage, their lives changed, and abundant blessings came their way.

Whether this is your first, second, or third marriage, it's not too late! There are six clear steps backed with Scripture that you can take to transform your marriage into the type of relationship God designed. First, though, make sure you're building your marriage on the firm foundation of Jesus Christ. Do you currently have a relationship with Christ? What does your faith walk currently look like? What are each of you doing for yourselves to feed and nourish your faith? What are you doing to feed and nourish your spouse's faith? These are important questions to ask yourself and discuss together as a couple. The more open and honest we are with each other about our faith and relationship with Christ, the better we can help each other in any areas in which we're struggling.

Matthew's Gospel exhorts us to "seek *first* the kingdom of God and his righteousness, and all these things will be added to you" (Matthew 6:33, emphasis added). When you start by focusing on the Lord and building your relationship on His firm foundation, a strong, healthy, and blessed marriage "will be added to you"—even if you have failed marriages in your past. It's never too late to experience the marriage of your dreams!

1. Pray together every day.

> The prayer of a righteous person has great power as it is working (James 5:16).

Numerous studies have found that only about 11 percent of couples pray together on a daily basis, but those who do have a staggeringly low divorce rate of *less than 1 percent!*[1] The most effective way to divorce-proof your marriage is to pray with your spouse. This is one of the most intense forms of intimacy, requiring complete trust and vulnerability with your husband or wife.

In addition to praying *with* your spouse, you should also be praying for your spouse every day. Prayer is the most powerful weapon we have in our arsenal against the enemy. It activates our marriage to come into alignment with Christ's heart and will for our relationship. In return, we can receive His grace, guidance, and direction for where He wants to take our marriage.

2. Be intentional in your communication.

> Let no corrupting talk come out of your mouths, but only such as is good for building up, as fits the occasion, that it may give grace to those who hear (Ephesians 4:29).

Communication is the cardiovascular system of your marriage. It carries the love, joy, partnership, support, and commitment from the beating heart of your marriage throughout the body of your family. Communication is a *life-or-death issue* for your marriage!

The way in which we speak to our spouse has the power to build them up or tear them down. What we say to them rarely reflects how we feel about them. Instead, how we speak to and treat our spouse is a direct reflection of how we see and feel about ourselves. Matthew 12:34 says, "For out of the abundance of the heart, the mouth speaks." The people we are closest to will reap the benefit or the destruction of what's in our heart.

Communication with our spouse requires patience, grace, love, and mutual respect. Choose to harness the power of communication in your marriage by being intentional about the time you spend simply talking to each other. Remember, your words have

---

[1] Lavern Nissley, "An Amazing Secret to Marriage Success," Encompass Connection Center, March 26, 2019, https://www.encompasscc.org/blog/an-amazing-secret-to-marriage-success.

power, and you must wield that power with grace and wisdom.

3. Recognize marriage as a faithful commitment to your spouse and to God.

> So they are no longer two but one flesh. What therefore God has joined together, let not man separate (Matthew 19:6).

Marriage is not just a contract between two people; it is an agreement, a *covenant* between God and His children. As soon as we say, "I do," our number-one responsibility (on earth) is to our spouse. They become the most important person on earth to us, such that we're called to love our spouse at least as much as we love ourselves (Ephesians 5:33).

Pledge to join together to create a new family dedicated to loving and serving the Lord both as individuals and as a team. Your family can do things for the Kingdom *together* that none of you could do alone. Your marriage is the beating heart of your family. When you allow that to suffer, your service to God suffers, so make a commitment to Him and to each other not to let that happen.

4. Forgive freely.

> [Bear] with one another and, if one has a complaint against another, [forgive] each other; as the Lord has forgiven you, so you also must forgive (Colossians 3:13).

No marriage is perfect, because no person is perfect. The question isn't whether we're going to do or say something that hurts our spouse; the question is what are we going to do about it when we inevitably do?

When we're hurt, we quickly fill up with resentment and anger. Left unchecked, that resentment will grow to consume our marriage. Proverbs 16:18 says, "Pride goes before destruction, and a haughty spirit before a fall." That's exactly what the enemy wants. He'll use anger, resentment, and pride to drive a wedge between you and your spouse. How do you stop him? You *forgive*. Forgiveness breaks the deadly separation the enemy uses to isolate a husband and wife from each other.

Forgiveness is not a passive activity. It requires a conversation. It means acknowledging the wrong that was done to us, giving grace, accepting the apology, and choosing to lay the issue down at the foot of the cross. (Of course, when an abusive spouse's actions put your physical, mental, or emotional safety at risk, you must still take appropriate steps to protect yourself and your children, even if you have a forgiving spirit.)

5. Show your spouse the same grace Christ has shown you.

> If anyone would come after me, let him deny himself and take up his cross daily and follow me (Luke 9:23).

A relationship that reflects God is one in which we surrender our marriage to Christ just like we're called to surrender ourselves: *every day*. It is not a one-time, bold moment of surrender and dying to self. It's an everyday act of giving our lives and marriage over to Him. In doing so, we're reminded of the fact that He loved us so much that He died to save us from sin. He gave His life so we could live with Him in perfect harmony for all eternity. What a beautiful picture of the sacrificial love we should strive for in our marriages!

Regardless of how severe our circumstances may be, the power of God can be made perfect in our weaknesses. The biggest and smallest mistakes are all opportunities for God to extend His limitless grace to you and your spouse and for the two of you to extend grace to each other. Grace for each other in marriage is what will carry us through both the difficult and the joyful times. It's what covers and protects us from the flaming arrows of the enemy and the lies he whispers in our ears about our spouse and marriage. A marriage that reflects God is a marriage that reflects God's grace.

6. Love with humility.

> God opposes the proud but gives grace to the humble (James 4:6).

The antidote to pride is humility. Humility is what God loves to see from His children, and it's an attitude He blesses in response. If you want riches, honor, and life in your marriage, it's time to set any trace of pride aside and cover yourself and your relationship in godly humility.

Mistakes don't have to ruin a marriage. In fact, your response to your spouse's mistakes could throw open the doors for a new wave of God's blessings to fall on your family. Humility, backed up by grace and forgiveness, does the impossible: it turns one step backward into two steps forward. In the face of trial or heartache, humility advances a marriage and brings spouses closer together.

Obviously, there's a big difference between showing your spouse humility and allowing yourself to be mistreated repeatedly. If that's the situation you're in, we strongly encourage you to seek the help of a pastor or professional marriage counselor. However, if you're like most of us and just bumping up against the unintended hurt feelings and frustrations of daily life with your spouse, we challenge you to walk through these six steps together as you work to improve your marriage and reflect God in your relationship.

There are concrete, practical steps you can take to protect your marriage and ensure your relationship reflects God's character. Decide on ground rules to protect your marriage from outside stressors and distractions. The following are things that work for us (Scott and Vanessa), and while they may or may not work for you, they should give you a good starting point for a discussion:

1. We will have intentional communication in the best communication style for the occasion.
2. We will not spend time alone with a member of the opposite sex.
3. We will have a full-transparency policy with each other.
4. We will be conscious of any behaviors that would make our spouse uncomfortable.
5. We will carefully guard our social media use.

None of the things we've "given up" are important enough to either of us to risk giving the enemy a foothold in our marriage. Our adherence to and comfort with these ground rules sets the tone for how others treat us and/or talk about our marriage. Feel free to use these ground rules or come up with something completely different. The goal is to identify what you, as a couple, are comfortable with, and then set guard rails in place to create that kind of life.

Learning and applying the disciplines discussed in this chapter don't come easy, especially if you don't take a heavenly perspective and God's-eye-view of your spouse. One of the hardest lessons I (Vanessa) had to learn as a wife is that I am not my husband's Holy Spirit. I spent years judging Scott for failing to live up to my unrealistic, imaginary picture of a perfect husband instead of honoring him for the incredible man God made him to be and the creation He continues to mold him into.

When we come to understand first who *we* are in the eyes of God, we can then begin to catch a glimpse of who our spouse really is. We can better understand why they do what they do and accept the fact that they're wired to do something different than what we're wired to do. That's how God made us—beautifully and wonderfully unique!

Your job isn't to change your spouse; your job is to see how their life reflects the work of their heavenly Father. Only when you can see the reflection of God in your spouse can you truly come together in a marriage that reflects God too.

RECOMMEND SCRIPTURE READING

He answered, "Have you not read that he who created them from the beginning made them male and female, and said, 'Therefore a man shall leave his father and his mother and hold fast to his wife, and the two shall become one flesh'? So they are no longer two but one flesh. What therefore God has joined together, let not man separate" (Matthew 19:4-6).

So God created man in his *own image*,
in the image of God he created him;
male and female he created them.
And God blessed them (Genesis 1:27-28, emphasis added).

No weapon that is fashioned against you shall succeed, and you shall refute every tongue that rises up against you in judgement. This is the heritage of the servants of the LORD, and their vindication from me, declares the LORD (Isaiah 54:17).

Choose this day whom you will serve ... But as for me and my house [family], we will serve the LORD (Joshua 24:15).

If anyone would come after me, let him deny himself and take up his cross daily and follow me (Luke 9:23).

An excellent wife is the crown of her husband,
but she who brings shame is like rottenness in his bones
(Proverbs 12:4).

DISCUSSION QUESTIONS

1. Why do you think couples sometimes feel awkward praying together? What can they do to overcome this awkwardness?

2. What are some ways you can be intentional in your communication with your spouse?

3. How would marriages change if we saw mistakes as opportunities to extend grace to our spouse?

4. Why does the world tend to bristle at godly ground rules in a relationship?

REFLECTION QUESTIONS

1. Does your marriage reflect God? If not, what or whom does it reflect?

2. How do you react when your spouse makes a mistake? Does this reaction line up with Scripture?

3. What ground rules, if any, do you have in your marriage? What ground rules do you wish you had, and what would it take to implement them?

PRAYER

Father God, we want our marriage to reflect You. We commit to spending time together in Your presence, and we also commit to being intentional in our communication with each other. We recognize that we are a team, and with Your help, our family will do amazing things! Please help us as we choose to forgive each other's faults and move forward in grace and humility. Give us wisdom as we establish ground rules that will protect our marriage and honor You. In Jesus' name, Amen.

ASSIGNMENT

- Read Chapter 5 in *Blended and Redeemed*.
- Ask the Lord, "What do You want to teach me?"

CHAPTER 5

THE FALSE PROMISE OF INNER VOWS

"When we make an inner vow, we aren't making a promise to ourselves at all. We're making a promise to the enemy."

ICEBREAKER
Besides your marriage vows, what is the best promise you ever made?

RECAP
There are six clear steps backed with Scripture that you can take to transform your marriage into the type of relationship God designed. First, pray together every day. Praying with your spouse puts a heavenly shield of protection around your marriage and your family. Second, be intentional in your communication. Your words have power, and you must wield that power with grace and wisdom. Third, recognize marriage as a faithful commitment to your spouse and to God. Your marriage is the beating heart of your family, and when you allow that to suffer, your service to God suffers too.

Fourth, forgive freely. Forgiveness means acknowledging the wrong that was done to us, giving grace, accepting the apology, and choosing to lay the issue down at the foot of the cross. Fifth, show your spouse the same grace Christ has shown you. Grace for each other in marriage is what will carry you through both the difficult and the joyful times. Sixth, love with humility. Your response to your spouse's mistakes could throw open the doors for a new wave of God's blessings to fall on your family.

Decide on ground rules to protect your marriage from outside stressors and distractions. The goal is to identify what you, as a couple, are comfortable with, and then set guard rails in place to create that kind of life. And remember, your job isn't to change your spouse but rather to see how their life reflects the work of their heavenly Father.

REVIEW

After we get hurt, especially going through something as painful as a divorce, we tend to not only bury our pain deep down, but we also make ourselves promises about what we will and/or won't do to prevent experiencing that kind of pain again. If we truly want to thrive in our new marriage and blended family, we've got to rummage through the damaged closets of our hearts and bring these deep-seated vows into the light of day, exposing it all.

When we're dating, most of us are always trying to put our best foot forward. It's almost like we're dressed up as the ideal version of ourselves—whom we want to be and how we want to be seen. Far too often, couples get to a point in the relationship where they feel as if they've disclosed just enough of what they want to share but not all of it. People can then put up a wall because they are ashamed or afraid to reveal the things behind it and because they are afraid of what the other person may think or feel about them. As long as the wall is up, they ignore the mess behind it and begin to move forward into the next season with an engagement and then marriage. They don't realize that at some point, their spouse is going to discover what's behind the wall, and that "mess" is going to have to be sorted through in order to clean it all up.

Once you get engaged, there's a sudden shift in focus. Dating is mostly about the present, and a little about the past, but the engagement is all about the future. It's about planning for the life you'll spend together—where you'll live, what you'll do, how many kids you want, and so on. The past is there, but it's not talked about much. You're "in the moment" with your eyes on the next moment. Then, boom! You're married and moving into your new home.

Within a few months, everything is perfect, set up exactly as you both want, and you're ready to start your new life together. That's when the doorbell rings. You go to the door to find two gigantic moving trucks parked across your lawn. You look at each other and ask, "What is all this?" As the movers start to unload the trucks, it hits you: this is all your baggage. You've got his-and-hers stockpiles of junk—all the emotional damage, memories, tears, arguments, bad moods, and trauma you stored away throughout your dating and engagement. Your ideal marriage suddenly gets messy, and neither of you are prepared for it.

Early in your marriage—usually within the first year—you will start to recognize things about your spouse you didn't know about. One of these discoveries can be self-made promises (inner vows) your spouse has made at some point in their life. By *inner vow*, we mean a promise forged in the heat of pain and loss. It's a declaration about what we will or won't do to protect ourselves from experiencing that kind of pain again. Inner vows start with I statements and are usually followed by "will never ..." or "will always ..."

These vows are meant to protect us. By doing this, we are making promises to ourselves, therefore trying to govern ourselves (instead of giving that control to God) to keep from getting hurt again. But they are false promises. We don't have the power to control the universe—that's God's job—and the only way to take that control for ourselves is to wrestle it out of God's hands. When we make inner vows, we make ourselves the protector and defender of our lives, thereby making ourselves the God over those areas. Inner vows serve to create a lack of trust between us and the Father, and that is the work of the enemy. Inner vows are more powerful than any of us could ever imagine, and when we think they are protecting us, they are actually limiting us to what we can receive from God.

The truth is, when we make an inner vow, we aren't making a promise to ourselves at all. We're making a promise to the enemy. The devil has been trying to convince us to reject God's control in our lives ever since the Garden of Eden (see Genesis 3). Control is pride, and pride is the pitfall of humanity—the very pitfall in which the enemy is trying to trap you.

Think of control as power. When we take power out of God's hands, we are basically handing it over to the enemy and allowing him to become more powerful. He twists our inner vows and uses them to hurt us in other ways. It's like he gets us laser focused on one thing so he can sneak around and attack us with something else. We don't see him coming on our left because he's tricked us into building a wall on our right.

It's often said that bitterness is a poison you prepare for someone else and then drink yourself. That's an apt description of inner vows, too. We make them in response to something someone else has done, but then they just sit there, taking up space in our hearts and eventually erecting walls ostensibly to protect us. Walls are indiscriminate; they keep bad things out, but they also keep out the good. The result is a stale, cold, lonely, and toxic stew of isolation we can sit in for years.

Nothing incites a slew of new inner vows like the trauma of divorce. That, of course, makes inner vows especially dangerous—and plentiful—in blended families. People often don't know what damage they have or what inner vows they've created after a divorce. It's like going through all the junk in a storage unit (or the moving van that shows up on your front lawn), finding a random item you haven't thought about in years, and exclaiming, "I didn't even know I still had this!"

People who've been through a divorce might be shocked to discover how much damage they're still carrying around with them years later, especially if they've "moved on" by remarrying, blending their family, and having more kids. A new marriage can be wonderful, but it isn't a magic cure-all that wipes away the hidden pain in your heart. It cannot and will not heal the deep wounds of a past divorce. That requires specific, time-consuming trauma work with the Great Physician and, most likely, a mental health professional.

Inner vows make us irrational and unteachable. They are based on feelings, not facts. That doesn't mean they're not "real," but it does mean they're usually not true. We come into agreement with a lie the enemy is telling us about a situation, and before long, we're giving the lie more control over our lives than we give God's truth. Our feelings are not always right or true, especially in moments where we are emotionally charged. We need God's Word to guide and direct us, because that is truth.

Inner vows make us unforgiving. "I will never and could never forgive my ex for what they did." Some people call that righteous indignation or justice, but in reality, it is a spirit of unforgiveness. There can be no *unforgiveness* in the Kingdom of God. Forgiveness is what Jesus is all about—it's why He came to earth. Refusing even the possibility of forgiveness is potentially the worst inner vow we can make. It keeps us tethered to the past for the rest of our lives.

Nothing feels more unnatural at the end of a bitter divorce, breakup, or litigation than asking God to give you a spirit of grace and forgiveness toward your ex. Forgiveness is hard, messy, and complicated, but to truly move forward and thrive in your life post-divorce, you've got to address any inner vows of unforgiveness.

Inner vows create landmines. Because you both come into the marriage with a truck full of past experiences, including inner vows you've never talked about (or may not even know about), you basically plant your marriage in the middle of a minefield. Everything looks great on the surface, but there are all these little landmines scattered everywhere, and you never know when you or your spouse will step on one. A landmine can be something you say, a habit you have, or something you might not think is a big deal but quickly discover is a huge deal to your spouse. You never even know the landmine is there, so there's no way to avoid it, and by the time you find out about it, it's already blown up in your face.

You must be intentional about "sweeping the minefield" early in your marriage, if not before. This will likely require some outside help, because many people don't even realize they have these landmines buried around. It's better to go looking for them intentionally rather than waiting until one blows up your marriage!

It's time to bring your inner vows out of the darkness and into the light of day so you and your spouse can finally deal with them and work through them. God's Word gives light to our lives and circumstances; it imparts understanding as we meditate on it and receive meaning and understanding from it (see Psalm 119:130). This is not an easy task, but it is immensely important, not only for your marriage but also for your physical, emotional, mental, and spiritual well-being.

How do you clear out a lifetime's worth of inner vows? **First, ask God to reveal your inner vows**. Examine yourself for any deep-seated conviction that might start with "I can't," "I won't," "This will not," or "I will never." Ask God to show you any area(s) where you might have put up walls around a trauma in an effort to protect yourself from future pain. Cry out like David:

> Search me, O God, and know my heart!
> Try me and know my thoughts!
> And see if there be any grievous way in me,
> and lead me in the way everlasting! (Psalm 139:23–24).

Second, repent of trying to take control away from God. By *repent*, we mean you must lay it down, turn your back to it, and walk away from it. Your inner vow is a lie made with the father of lies. It was never of God, so it is time to lay it at the feet of Jesus and be done with it forever.

Third, renounce your inner vow. Surrender it fully to God and give control of that area of your life back to Him. Here, you're replacing the inner vow with a new declaration of God's control, power, and blessing in your life. Proverbs 28:13 declares, "Whoever conceals their sins does not prosper, but the one who confesses and renounces them finds mercy" (NIV).

Fourth, forgive the person who hurt you. This might sound irrational—maybe even impossible—especially if the person is unrepentant. You might feel inclined to hold on to your pain, thinking your ex or whoever else hurt you doesn't *deserve* your forgiveness. This is where our inner vows can keep us stuck for years or even decades. The enemy doesn't want us to forgive because he'd rather keep us trapped in our own pain and suffering for as long as possible. He also knows forgiveness is a reflection of Christ.

Luke 6:37 says, "Forgive, and you will be forgiven." Our response to God forgiving us should include our willingness to forgive *others*. In fact, we may never look more like Christ than when we forgive those who have hurt us. Forgiveness does not always mean relational reconciliation, but it does mean freeing yourself from the weight of your unforgiveness and truly wanting the best for the other person. It's not up to you to determine what that "best" looks like—that's between them and God. Your only goal here is breaking free of the inner vow and unforgiveness that have kept you tied to this source of pain for too long.

There is freedom from inner vows. There is healing. There is restoration. It may not come immediately, and it most certainly won't come easily. It may take a lot of reliance on the Lord, getting into His presence with daily Bible reading, prayer, and possibly counseling. God is bigger than your pain, and He has more power than your inner vow. You can be free.

RECOMMEND SCRIPTURE READING

Search me, O God, and know my heart!
Try me and know my thoughts!
And see if there be any grievous way in me,
and lead me in the way everlasting! (Psalm 139:23–24).

If you abide in my word ... you will know the truth, and the truth will set you free (John 8:31–32).

All Scripture is breathed out by God and profitable for teaching, for reproof, for correction, and for training in righteousness, that the man of God may be complete, equipped for every good work (2 Timothy 3:16–17).

Be kind to one another, tenderhearted, *forgiving one another, as God in Christ forgave you* (Ephesians 4:32, emphasis added).

Whoever conceals their sins does not prosper, but the one who confesses and renounces them finds mercy (Proverbs 29:13 NIV).

And whenever you stand praying, forgive, if you have anything against anyone, so that your Father also who is in heaven may forgive you your trespasses (Mark 11:25).

DISCUSSION QUESTIONS

1. What would the world consider a "normal" reaction to pain?

2. How does this differ from what Scripture says?

3. How is an inner vow a false promise?

4. Explain this statement: "Walls are indiscriminate—they keep the bad things out, but they also keep out the good."

5. What are some ways unforgiveness takes control over people's lives?

REFLECTION QUESTIONS

1. What "landmines" are lurking in your marriage? What can you do to disarm them?

2. Think of one person or situation that you've struggled to forgive. How do you think it would feel to be free from unforgiveness?

3. Ask the Lord, "What do You want me to do about my inner vows?"

_____

_____

_____

_____

PRAYER

Father God, we admit that we have made inner vows in response to the pain we've experienced in life. Please forgive us for trying to take control away from You and for listening to the lies of the enemy. Today, we renounce every inner vow, and by faith, we choose to forgive the people who have hurt us. Thank You, Lord, for the freedom that comes from knowing and submitting to You. We trust You, and we believe that You have good plans for our lives. In Jesus' name, Amen.

ASSIGNMENT

- Read Chapter 6 in *Blended and Redeemed*.
- Ask the Lord, "What do You want to teach me?"

CHAPTER 6

BLENDING YOUR BUNCH

"You may not love your biological children and stepchildren exactly the same way, but you can love them with same intensity and intentionality."

ICEBREAKER
What is your favorite thing about your children?

RECAP
Inner vows are self-made promises that declare what we will or won't do to protect ourselves from experiencing pain again. When we make an inner vow, we're really trying to take control away from God and making a promise to the enemy at the same time. Inner vows make us irrational, unteachable, and unforgiving, and they create relational landmines.

To clear out inner vows, begin by asking God to reveal them to you. Ask Him to show you any area(s) where you might have put up walls around a trauma in an effort to protect yourself from future pain. Then repent of the inner vow and ask God to forgive you for trying to take away His lordship and sovereignty in your life. Renounce your vow—surrender it fully to God and give control of that area of your life back to Him. Finally, forgive the person who hurt you. Forgiveness does not always mean relational reconciliation, but it does mean freeing yourself from the weight of unforgiveness and truly wanting the best for the other person.

REVIEW
Love comes in many forms and types. You may not feel the same type of love for your stepchildren as you do for your biological

children, and that okay! You have a deep history with your biological children that goes far beyond genetics, which is a wonderful, beautiful thing—and something you likely don't have with your stepchildren, depending on when you came into their lives. This rich and complex history molds how we love our children. The question isn't really, *Will I love my stepchildren the same way I love my biological children?* The real question is, *Can I love my stepchildren just as **intensely** as I love my biological children?* And the answer to that is a resounding yes!

Love is a gift from God. It is born of Him, flows from Him, and produces rich fruit in our lives. Love is not only from God, but God also is love, and He enables us to love. The power and intensity of love come from God, not from our genetics nor our personal history with someone. You may not love your biological children and stepchildren exactly the same way, but you can love them with same intensity and intentionality. This is what Scripture calls sacrificial love, which you'll often hear referred to by the Greek term *agape*. This is the type of love Paul describes in 1 Corinthians 13:4-8, which you've probably heard quoted at every wedding you've ever attended.

> Love is patient and kind; love does not envy or boast; it is not arrogant or rude. It does not insist on its own way; it is not irritable or resentful; it does not rejoice at wrongdoing, but rejoices with the truth. Love bears all things, believes all things, hopes all things, endures all things.
>
> Love never ends.

This kind of love—the highest of the four types of love mentioned in the Bible—is the goal for *every* parent, whether they're natural, step, or otherwise.

It is okay that the love you feel for your stepchild is different than the love you feel for your biological child. It doesn't make you a bad stepparent, a bad spouse, or a bad human being. You can love them *differently* and still love them *equally*, though that doesn't happen accidentally or automatically. It requires a choice to love sacrificially, and it requires you to back that choice up with your most precious commodity: your time.

Children spell *love* "t-i-m-e." They want your time and energy, and they want that time and energy focused on them. This is never more important than in the early stages of establishing a strong base for your stepparent-stepchild relationship. Shortchanging quality one-on-one time with your new stepchildren at this stage can leave you with a cracked and weak relational foundation that could one day bring the whole thing crashing down around you.

Kingdom relationships are built through loving the Father and abiding in Him, and by this, love is perfected through us. First John 4:18 says, "There is no fear in love, but perfect love casts out fear." If you ever doubt or have insecurities about loving and cultivating a relationship with your stepchildren, know that this is not the will of the Father, but rather a tactic of the enemy to devise separation between you and your stepchildren. God has strategically handpicked and equipped you to be their stepparent. When we love God, His love is perfected in us, so God is perfecting His love in and through us as we love our stepchildren.

It's perfectly natural to hit obstacles and want to back off, thinking there will be time to build a relationship later. Here's the thing, though: you're *already* building a relationship whether you're trying to or not. The only difference is that by not spending intentional time with the child, you're building a weak relationship—one you'll have to spend even more time trying to rebuild later on. Spending time with the child on the front end of your relationship is an investment that will yield unimaginable dividends for the rest of your life.

So what do you do with the time you've set aside for the child? That's up to you! It can come down to a lot of different factors such as age, interests, and gender (yours and theirs). Start by simply meeting the child where they are. Get involved in the things they like and ask the Holy Spirit to show you things about them (even things they do not know about themselves) so you can encourage them from a heavenly perspective. No matter how crazy life gets, how busy you are, or how many children you have in the house, nothing will do more to build a long-lasting, loving relationship of trust and parent-child bonding than spending time together—as a family, one on one, and, most importantly, with Jesus. If there are multiple kids in the mix, you will want to be sure to spend equal time with each of them. Get to know each child as the wonderful, beautiful individual he or she is, and give them the time they need to get to know (and love) their new mom or dad.

Don't just sit around waiting and hoping for a deeper connection. Be intentional! Get in there, be active, and learn how to best love each other while doing things together. Kids build relationship in the context of activities and having fun, so make sure you're providing those opportunities.

One of the most common questions new blended couples ask is, "What should the child call their new stepparent?" Our answer is both simple and complicated: *whatever they want*. Giving them the option is important for a couple of reasons. First, it takes the anxiety of your expectations off their shoulders as they're trying to navigate this new reality. Children like to please their parents, and they'll often make decisions based on what they think their parents want.

Second, letting the child choose the name helps them own an important part of their relationship with the new stepparent. Names are important, and the opportunity to choose a name for someone is especially powerful. By giving children the opportunity to decide for themselves what to call the stepparent, you're giving them a tiny piece of control and allowing them to take the first step towards establishing a relationship with their stepparent. Plus, you're giving yourself the gift of insight into how your child sees their new stepparent.

The name a child chooses to give their new stepparent affects their other biological parent more than anyone else. As the biological parent, understand that what the child calls the stepparent does not change or diminish your role in any way. Yes, it feels very personal, sometimes even like a betrayal, but it's simply the child trying to categorize his or her relationships appropriately. The hardest thing for a parent to do in this situation is to lay down their pride and give their child space to make these critical decisions that will set the tone for their future relationship with the stepparent.

Many couples enter a new marriage with unrealistic expectations about how quickly and easily their children will adjust to all the changes. It's important to remember that your blended family relationship isn't a sprint—it's a marathon, and you're doing it as a team. The first step is to lay down any expectations you might have about what those relationships are going to look like and how quickly it's going to happen. The best you can do is ensure you're creating a safe, secure atmosphere in which healthy parent and sibling relationships can flourish ... and then wait. Relationships happen organically. Trying to force things to happen prematurely can change the character of the relationship and the blessings the Lord wants to do in it.

Of course, that doesn't mean there aren't some things you can do to create the best possible conditions for new relationships to develop. Find ways to put the *fun* in the *dysfunctional* moments. It can be unreasonable to expect children to go from strangers to siblings overnight. That's a huge expectation that not many people can accomplish. They need to get to know each other, and the best way for them to do that is to connect as they do fun things together. What are some fun "family dates" you can set up for your bunch? What does everyone like doing? In what situations do your kids let their guards down a little bit? Be intentional about identifying those things and then pack your schedule with opportunities for your family to truly blend. When your kids know what to expect, they can start to "give in" to the new flow and structure of the family. That provides the safe, stable foundation they need to thrive.

Be creative in making daily and weekly touchpoints for your family. Time together builds connection, and routines create stability. Having at least one time per day when everyone is at the same place at the same time is priceless. Other possibilities for family touchpoints include daily prayer, weekly game or move nights, and yearly vacations.

One important thing that brings families together is a rich history of family traditions. Creating family traditions gives your family something truly unique, something only those "in the know" can understand. These are the things that cement "family memories" in our minds. You and your kids need that—especially in a blended family when you're all coming together from different family traditions. Figure out what works for your family in your specific custody situation and make it a tradition. These are the moments you and your kids will always remember. These are the things they'll talk about when they're old and gray, long after you're gone. Give them those memories and traditions! Give them things they can always point to and say, "This is *ours*."

Be sure all the grandparents and the rest of the extended family are involved with your blended family. Talk to the grandparents, aunts, uncles, and cousins. Tell them how important it is to you and to your children that they have the full love and support of the *whole* family. Make sure they have all the children's birthdays on their calendars and that they are showing equal love through the words and attention they give your kids.

Blending a family is a lot like mixing a cake. You and your spouse are the eggs—because you're equally yoked (pun intended). Your children are the sugar, cocoa, flour, nuts, and chocolate chips. The traditions and times you spend together are the oil—the glue that holds everything together. The joy you share is the icing on top. And Jesus is the baking pan that holds it all together in one place—poured out to completion.

RECOMMENDED SCRIPTURE READING

Behold, how good and pleasant it is
when brothers dwell in unity! (Psalm 133:1).

Beloved, let us love one another, *for love is from God*, and whoever loves has been born of God and knows God. Anyone who does not love does not know God, because God is love (1 John 4:7–8, emphasis added).

Love is patient and kind; love does not envy or boast; it is not arrogant or rude. It does not insist on its own way; it is not irritable or resentful; it does not rejoice at wrongdoing, but rejoices with the truth. Love bears all things, believes all things, hopes all things, endures all things.
Love never ends (1 Corinthians 13:4–8).

There is no fear in love, but perfect love casts out fear (1 John 4:18).

DISCUSSION QUESTIONS

1. How can stepparents show sacrificial love to their stepchildren?

   _____

   _____

   _____

   _____

2. Why is it important to spend time together as a family, even if a stepchild seems to dislike the new parent?

   _____

   _____

   _____

   _____

3. What are some fun activities families can do together to help stepsiblings connect and bond?

4. Why is it important to have the support and love of extended family members?

REFLECTION QUESTIONS

1. How much time and energy are you putting into your relationship with all your children?

2. What are your feelings about the "name talk"? Is there anything in your heart that you need to confess and release to the Lord?

3. What three words would you like to describe your family in five years?

_____

_____

_____

_____

PRAYER

Father God, thank You for bringing us together as a beautiful, blended family. We can love each other because You first loved us. Please help us use our time and energy wisely for the benefit of our family. Forgive us when we make mistakes, and remind us to extend grace to one another. May our children always know that we love them, and may our home be a place of peace and rest. In Jesus' name, Amen.

ASSIGNMENT

- Read Chapter 7 in *Blended and Redeemed*.
- Ask the Lord, "What do You want to teach me?"

CHAPTER 7

PARENTING AND CO-PARENTING

"No matter how different your two families are, you will always have one thing in common: your child."

ICEBREAKER

What is your family's favorite sport to watch or play?

RECAP

You may not love your biological children and stepchildren exactly the same way, but through God, you can love them with same *intensity* and *intentionality*. Children spell *love* "t-i-m-e." God has strategically handpicked and equipped you to be their stepparent, and nothing will do more to build a long-lasting, loving relationship of trust and parent-child bonding than spending time together.

By giving your children the opportunity to decide for themselves what to call the stepparent, you're giving them a tiny piece of control and allowing them to take the first step towards establishing a relationship with their stepparent. Plus, you're giving yourself the gift of insight into how your child sees their new stepparent.

Find ways to put the *fun* in the *dysfunctional* moments. Time together builds connection, and routines create stability. Create new family traditions and memories that your children can point to and say, "This is ours." Involve the extended family and make sure everyone knows how important it is that your children have the full love and support of the whole family.

REVIEW

Co-parenting is a team sport, but sometimes it feels as if our teammates are more like the opponents playing against us. The blessing is that there should already be a partnering plan in place, which both parties have either agreed to or a judge has filed within the legal system. This is a great place to start building the trust in your co-parenting relationship and possibly navigating toward a better situation for both parents and the child(ren). As things develop in your co-parenting relationship or as the children age, you can alter your plan as needed. Your custody orders or decree can be a great starting point of a successful co-parenting relationship with your ex, but if it is not possible (now or later on) you at least have a support plan to use.

The first practical obstacle we must face in working on a healthy co-parenting relationship is **basic communication.** The single most important rule when it comes to communicating with your ex in a co-parenting relationship is also the rule most blended families break on a regular basis: parents should *never* communicate through the child. This goes for any kind of communication, whether it's something as innocuous as scheduling issues or something much more confrontational.

When you make the child the messenger, you are putting a mountain of stress and anxiety on their little shoulders—a burden they were never meant to bear. This makes the child feel like they must choose a side. They don't want to make either parent upset, and because the adults in the room either can't or don't want to work with each other, they put all that responsibility on the child. This is the worst possible option we can choose. Such pressure and stress on a child can lead to chronic anxiety, depression, and behavioral issues.

Ex-spouses generally don't want or need to spend an hour on the phone every night catching up on the events of the day, but we are called to live in peace with and edify one another (see Romans 14:19). The frequency of your communication with your child's other parent will vary based on your situation and the age of the child, but you should still have one-on-one chats at least a couple times a month. With younger children, it may be wiser to talk to your ex at least once a week. Touching base once a week, even for just a few minutes, gives each parent the chance to update the other on what's going on, how things are going in school, scheduling issues, disciplinary issues, behavioral issues, health issues, and so on. Having these weekly calls or emails on your schedule also prevents either of you from accidentally falling into the habit of using your child as a messenger.

Plan on a longer, more detailed planning meeting two to four times a year. Quarterly meetings might work on the high end; semi-annual meetings (such as around New Year's and the start of the school year) could be an option on the low end. Plan on more time for these calls, and you might even want to include the stepparents as well, just to make sure each family is on the same page. For these longer meetings, you should discuss long-term (three to six months) family plans like vacations, holidays, financial matters, school events, etc. This is a good time to pull up whatever shared calendar or planning tools you might use together and make sure everything is up to date and accounted for.

We understand that talking to your ex *at all* may simply be impossible. In those cases, we recommend relying on tech-based communication tools like shared calendars and online planning apps to aid you in your season. There are many wonderful planning services designed specifically for blended families and divorced spouses. In fact, your divorce decree might even specify a recommended solution. These tools do a great job of coordinating schedules, giving you a place to store documents like receipts and medical papers, a way to transfer money for reimbursements, a daily journal that no one can view other than you and your ex-spouse, and so on.

Another option when the relationship between the biological parents is strained is to let the stepparent interface with the other biological parent. Stepparents often have to ride a fine line between respecting the other parent as the child's mom or dad and protecting their own spouse from a potentially toxic relationship with their ex. You may need your spouse to own the communication channel long-term, or you might need to give up one-on-one communication altogether and rely solely on other family planning tools. Even if you need to change methods from time to time, strive for consistency and quality communication through whatever system works best for you.

If the other parent will not respond to you or participate in any communication methods whatsoever, it is still important for you to fulfill your obligations, especially those outlined in the divorce decree. In these situations, since you aren't talking by phone or in person, you'll be interacting almost exclusively through written communication—even if you never receive a response. The good news is that this makes it super easy to keep a record of every piece of communication. In the worst-case scenario, you want to be able to show that you've done everything in your power to maintain a healthy co-parenting relationship.

Even the best children need correction from time to time, and this can present special challenges for a blended family. We've developed a basic five-point plan for disciplining children in a blended family:

1. **The biological parent takes the lead.**
   In a blended family, it's always a good idea to let the biological parent take the lead in disciplining the child—especially at first. In the early days of a new blended family, the child still getting to know and trust the stepparent, and this trust-building can be jeopardized by the stepparent taking disciplinary action too soon.
2. **Parents present a united front.**
   There are times in every family, blended or not, when one parent doesn't fully understand the other parent's actions. There is nothing wrong with one parent disagreeing with the other's disciplinary action—as long as those disagreements are discussed privately. Children need to see that their

parents are on the same page regarding discipline.

3. **Both biological parents are on the same page (if possible).**
Guard your family from the possibility of the child playing one biological parent against the other. The only way to do this is to communicate with the child's other biological parent regularly about disciplinary issues and general behavioral guidelines the child should follow in both homes. As new behavioral challenges come up, do your best to have an open and honest discussion with the other parent.

4. **Serious disciplinary issues are communicated to the other parent.**
Whether the other biological parent is actively participating in the disciplinary issues you've discussed with them, you still need to update them regularly on any major behavioral problems you've experienced with the child. This is another opportunity to avoid having the child play one parent against the other, and it also shows respect to the other parent by giving them a head's up on a potential new behavioral problem.

5. **Drop-off day disciplinary issues are not "free passes."**
It would be ideal for both biological parents to agree on the same discipline regardless of whose weekend it is, but realistically you cannot expect the other parent to ground the child on their time for you. You'll usually need to set a reasonable expectation with the child for when they get home. Inform the other parent about what happened so he or she can watch out for similar behavioral issues.

Raising kids is expensive. Food, shelter, clothes, healthcare, daycare, school, sports, extracurricular activities, a little fun here and there ... This all begins to add up, and it is a lot! When the two biological parents are living in different households, effective financial management for the child's needs requires an extra layer of communication and teamwork.

If you are expected per your custody orders to pay child support, then make it a priority in your household budget. Budgeting and making your child support payments on time, every time, is not only a gift to your child but will also bless your marriage more than you realize. You want to make sure you are managing your money well enough to honor your obligation to your child, and your spouse needs to be on board with your commitment to do right by your child. Sure, it can be hard to hand that check to your ex every month, but you can try to stop thinking about it as handing it to your ex. What you're really doing is giving your child the money they need to live a rich, full life. Our children depend on us, and it's our duty—our *joy*—to do our best to support them. When we fulfill our child support agreements, we honor both our children and the Lord.

We know there are situations in which one biological parent can take advantage of the other parent and child, abusing the use of child support and using it for things not related to the child. We want to encourage you not to lose hope and to continue to place your faith in the Lord. Trust Him to provide for your needs and your child's needs. After praying through the matter, you may find that the best (or only) solution is to seek legal counsel. Be sure you're documenting *everything*—every email, text, conversation, and missed child-support payment. Sadly, you'll need records of all of it if you end up back in court.

Your commitment to fulfill your child support obligation needs the full cooperation of your spouse. The Bible says you and your spouse are *one flesh*. We believe that one flesh equals *one budget*. If one of you has a big financial commitment, the other shares in that commitment. That means your child support payments will play a significant part in your family's monthly budget.

It is absolutely critical to make sure your partner understands the importance and priority of this commitment before you get married. You must be on the same page with your finances and understand that your child support payments will be a reality in your married life together. It's a critical conversation every engaged couple needs to have before starting a new blended family. Be up front with your partner about this, work out a budgeting plan together, talk through it, lay out your struggles with this, and discuss any concerns you may have and how this will impact your family financially.

We also encourage you to talk about how much good this will do for the child and even where you can provide extra help beyond what's outlined in the agreement. Our parenting is not limited to the monthly payment we owe or the weekend we have custody. It is a role we are actively participating in all the time. The Lord will honor your faithfulness to do more. If you see your ex struggling financially even though you are sending them the "right amount" of child support, pray and ask the Lord if there is anything else He would like you to do for them.

The biggest question we've heard from parents who receive support payments from the child's other parent is, "Do we have to allocate every dollar of this to a specific expense for the child, or should this money simply flow into our normal monthly budget as income?" We know families who do it both ways. One lesson we have learned in these situations is that "good paper makes for better friends (or circumstances)." Whatever the case may be in your situation, start by asking the Lord how He wants you to do it. Then, if you have an amicable relationship with your ex, maybe you can sit down together and have a thorough conversation about this. If you do not have a good relationship with your ex, you should at least do this with your spouse and come up with a plan and budget that works best for your home.

The more traditional—and we might add, *reasonable*—way we've seen couples do this is to simply flow that money into your household budget as income and then make sure you're taking care of the child's needs to a reasonable extent. If there are any leftover funds from what you've received, we recommend tossing them into a college fund or some other financial fund that will benefit the child later in life.

Ideally, the support payments outlined in the divorce decree are only the starting point. It's great if you and your ex can go beyond the court-mandated support arrangement and team up to pay various child-related expenses together. As children get older, their financial needs change in ways not always reflected in the decree. This is when you need to have clear and honest communication with your ex to make sure you're sharing the load of rearing your child. You can work together to identify what makes sense for your child and your families. This is an exercise in working together for the good of the child and for one another in your co-parenting relationship. It builds trust, and trust establishes healthy relationships, which pours straight into the children. It is a win for everyone.

Many co-parenting families are as different as night and day and may not have anything in common with each other financially, professionally, socially, or spiritually. However, no matter how different your two families are, you will always have one thing in common: your child. You don't have to share interests or hang out together, and there is no expectation that you should have to. What you want to do is work together to raise this child into the world-changing Kingdom agent God created them to be.

Parenting is a team sport. The biblical ideal points to both the mother's and father's roles in raising a child. God designed families to have a mom and a dad working together in raising the child. Our goal should always be to live up to and honor that standard—even when it's hard.

RECOMMEND SCRIPTURE READING

My son, keep your father's commandment,
and forsake not your mother's teaching.
Bind them on your heart always;
tie them around your neck.
When you walk, they will lead you;
when you lie down, they will watch over you;
and when you awake, they will talk with you
(Proverbs 6:20–22).

No discipline seems pleasant at the time, but painful. Later on, however, it produces a harvest of righteousness and peace for those who have been trained by it (Hebrews 12:11 NIV).

So then we pursue the things which make for peace and the building up of one another (Romans 14:19 NASB).

Pay to all what is owed to them: taxes to whom taxes are owed, revenue to whom revenue is owed, respect to whom respect is owed, honor to whom honor is owed (Romans 13:7).

It is more blessed to give than to receive (Acts 20:35).

DISCUSSION QUESTIONS

1. How can biological parents help relieve the pressure their children feel in a co-parenting situation?

   _____

   _____

   _____

   _____

2. What forms of healthy communication have you seen work well for blended families?

   _____

   _____

   _____

   _____

3. How can a stepparent support the biological parent when it comes to discipline?

   _____

   _____

4. Child support can be a hot topic in blended families. How should believers respond, whether on the giving or receiving end?

REFLECTION QUESTIONS

1. What is one step you can take to improve your coparenting communication?

2. What boundaries do you need to begin enforcing in order to help your children experience consistency, routine, and structure in your home?

3. How can you celebrate and encourage your child's relationship with their other parent?

_____

_____

_____

_____

PRAYER

Father God, our desire is to have the best co-parenting relationship possible. Give us wisdom as we learn how to communicate in healthy, productive ways. Protect our children's hearts and minds. Let us set the example of receiving correction with open, humble hearts. Lord, everything we have comes from You, and we commit to stewarding our resources with honor and integrity. In Jesus' name, Amen.

ASSIGNMENT

- Read Chapter 8 in *Blended and Redeemed*.
- Ask the Lord, "What do You want to teach me?"

CHAPTER 8

FACING NEW FAMILY CHALLENGES TOGETHER

*"Don't let fear drive your thoughts and actions;
let your faith drive them."*

ICEBREAKER

Where was your favorite place to hang out as a child or teenager?

RECAP

The three key areas of a healthy co-parenting relationship are communication, discipline, and financial partnership. Never communicate through your children, because this puts a great burden of stress and anxiety on them. Instead, find a way to have quality communication that is consistent and direct and that complies with your divorce decree.

Discipline can present special challenges for blended families, so it's a good idea to let the biological parent take the lead, especially at the beginning. Children need to see their parents on the same page regarding discipline, and if possible, the other biological parent should be informed of any serious disciplinary issues. Children also need to know that drop-off day disciplinary issues are not "free passes," and there will be appropriate consequences when they return to your home.

If you are expected to pay child support, then make it a priority in your budget. When you fulfill your child support agreement, you honor both your children and the Lord. If you receive child support, ask the Lord how He wants you to manage child-related expenses. Then come up with a plan and budget that works best for your home and coincides with your custody papers.

REVIEW

Divorce is never easy. It can leave you feeling rejected, bitter, shameful, and hopeless. If you have a child with your ex, then you can't escape each other entirely when the dust settles. You'll have to communicate regularly on some level at least until the child turns 18, and even then, you'll most likely have to interact occasionally, such as at weddings and future grandchildren's birthday parties.

How you interact with your ex is up to you, but your attitude *about* them and *around* them will have long-lasting implications for everyone involved. Who is going to pay the biggest price if you have a terrible attitude about your ex? Your child. It's not your best for them, nor is it God's. You can model the character of Christ by having an attitude of kindness toward your ex, even if it is not reciprocated. His kindness leads us to repentance (Romans 2:4). By doing this, you can save yourself and your kids even more pain than you've already experienced.

Learning how to guard your heart and attitude when it comes to working with, talking to, and talking *about* your ex-spouse may not be easy, but it's a discipline, and when we practice this daily, God will honor our obedience. Proverbs 4:23 declares, "Above all else, guard your heart, for everything you do flows from it" (NIV). What we choose to believe and think about our ex affects our minds and hearts. It will flow out of us as a blessing or a curse, so we must guard our hearts for the spiritual and physical well-being of our children and relationships.

Most parents are so focused on their own household and the urgent needs in front of them that they can miss one important detail: you are a part of *one* blended family, but your child is a part of *two*. Helping them truly feel "at home" at both places and always connected to their other parent is a serious challenge that requires some coordination between households. The good news is that making your child more comfortable in their back-and-forth way of life is something that's easily fixed with just a little attention to two things: accommodations and communication.

Most children in blended families have two of everything: two sets of parents, two sets of siblings, two households, two bedrooms, and if we're not careful, two completely separate worlds. This can be incredibly jarring for a child who's always switching back and forth. Too often, going to the other parent's home on the weekends feels more like staying at a hotel than going to "my other home." You want to actively work against this. The child needs to feel at home in both places—and that's not going to happen without some parental intentionality.

We encourage you to ask your child(ren) lots of questions, such as:

- What can we do to help you feel more at home in both places?
- What are you struggling with that we can try to fix?
- What would make the transition easier on the weekends and summers?
- What are we not seeing that you'd like us to know about?
- What makes one place feel more like "home" than the other?
- What do you miss at one house that you have at the other?

There are simple changes you can make that go a long way to making your child feel completely comfortable, safe, accepted, and wanted. Identify what those things are and communicate them to the other parent. Having these conversations and finding solutions goes a long way to making the transition period easy for children initially and gives them a true sense of *home* at both places for the long term.

Another area sometimes overlooked is the child's easy access to communication with the other parent. We've heard parents say time and time again, "When my child is with me, it's my time—not my ex's time." It's almost as if one parent is trying to cut the other one out of the loop, at least for a weekend or for a few weeks over the summer. Do not fall into this trap! It's a tactic from the enemy, and it will not give you a better experience with your child. In fact, it will likely do just the opposite.

Wherever the child is, they never stop having *two* parents. You need to be sure to facilitate good communication between the child and the other parent when they are with you. For young children, communication tools may include a landline telephone, a cell phone, an iPad (or tablet), or other tech-based solutions. Whatever you and your ex decide on, just accept the fact that you are responsible for helping them stay in touch when the child is young.

It's more common for teens to have their own cell phones so they can "own" the responsibility of staying in touch with their other parent when they're apart. If you need to ground your child from their phone, don't take it away before you work with the other parent to figure out a clear, dependable means of communication between the two of them. Grounding a teenager from their phone should *not* mean grounding them from talking to their other parent!

A more important and yet much more evasive and insidious challenge is the issue of child manipulation and parent alienation. This is one of the most common things we hear from blended families, but it's something almost no one talks about. Divorce decrees and planning apps do a great job at helping parents figure out the practical details of co-parenting a child, but these tools don't do anything to help parents learn how to *emotionally* work together. Parents who can't identify and eliminate child manipulation and parent alienation tactics—both in their ex-partner and in themselves—will always struggle with the co-parenting dynamic. Even worse, they'll unknowingly bring incredible harm to their own children.

Child manipulation involves the ways a parent tries to control a child's thoughts or feelings. This can be done directly or indirectly and intentionally or unintentionally. Oftentimes, a parent doesn't even know they're doing it.

Alienation is the attempt to isolate someone from another person or group. Sometimes, alienation can be a good thing, such as when we keep our children away from obviously bad influences or dangerous people. However, parent alienation is the negative and selfish act of manipulating a child to dislike or cut off the other parent relationship.

Psychologist Murray Bowen famously described emotional systems like this as triangles with three points:

1. **The Alienating Parent:** The parent seeking to separate the child from the other parent, stepparent, and/or blended family.
2. **The Target Child:** The child who is being targeted to elicit negative behaviors toward and emotions about the other parent, while also isolating them.
3. **The Target Parent:** The parent you want to affect.

The goal of this process is the total isolation and alienation of the target parent and to completely demolish his or her parent-child relationship with the child you share.

We've seen so many children who've grown to despise one parent because they were led (or groomed) to believe lie after lie, taking on the emotional pain and trauma of one parent against the other. It's heartbreaking, and it can have long-term effects on the mental, emotional, and spiritual well-being of the child.

What causes child manipulation and parent alienation? First and foremost, we must realize that the enemy is working against all of us. He hates our families, and he'll use our pain, our thoughts, and even our love and concern for our children against us if we let him.

A blended family is usually preceded by the loss or ending of a relationship, either a divorce or a breakup between two loving partners. These are seasons of devastation for heartbroken adults, and they come with a wide range of emotional responses. There's a huge amount of fear involved in the dissolution of a marriage. Fear makes us irrational, and it will make us do and say things we never thought we would. Then add feelings of rejection, regret, and shame that inevitably follow a divorce or serious breakup, and the emotional burden compounds exponentially.

The apostle Paul wrote, "God gave us a spirit not of fear but of power and love and self-control" (2 Timothy 1:7). We can rest in knowing that we were created to be strong and courageous, and despite the fact that we may have ended up in a situation where divorce was the outcome, we do not have to be fearful about our future circumstances. Our Father goes with us, and He will never leave or forsake us (see Deuteronomy 31:6; Hebrews 13:5).

Of course, sharing custody of a child means there's no chance of a "clean break," because you still have this connective tissue—your child—keeping you tethered to your ex. You love your child, but he or she is still a walking, talking reminder of the lost relationship that's caused so much pain. We can become terrified of losing our closest remaining relationship—our child—to the person for whom we have all these painful, complicated emotions. In response, we can instinctively seek to alienate the child from our ex. If we were to stop and think about it, we might justify it as "protecting" the child from someone we've deemed untrustworthy and dangerous. In reality, though, it's more likely that we're lashing out in pain and fear. Don't let fear drive your thoughts and actions; let your faith drive them.

Fear is not from God. Doubt, pain, rejection, and shame are also not from God. Those are weapons of the enemy, a few of the "flaming darts" Ephesians 6:16 warns us against. There is a spiritual war raging all around us, and we must be aware of our enemy to withstand his schemes. In the case of blended families, he's already attacked a previous relationship that ended in a divorce or breakup, and we cannot be so naïve to think that he's not going to come after our new family as well. As Paul wrote in a letter to the Corinthians, we must strive to "not be outwitted by Satan; for we are not ignorant of his designs" (2 Corinthians 2:11).

In a triangulation relationship, one or both parents can intentionally or unknowingly convince the child that their other parent is "bad." This puts a huge burden on the child that inevitably turns into anxiety, which expresses itself in a number of symptoms, including depression, guilt, anger, and isolation. More importantly, it can lead to an iron-clad root of bitterness that will affect their chances for a quality life forever. Bitterness is a poison that spreads resentment to the people around us and pursues the opposite of peace and holiness. This is what we're handing our children when we try to alienate them from their other parent. Whether we do it as a way to punish our ex or protect our child, the result is usually the same: we gravely harm the child by piling damage on top of an already difficult situation.

Step one in our recovery from engaging in alienating behavior is to do a thorough "heart exam" on ourselves. We must stop pointing the finger at our ex and examine our own thoughts, behaviors, and feelings. Ask God to reveal anything in your heart that is not of Him and show you if you have been acting or thinking in a way that could be alienating your child from their other parent.

Second, ask God to forgive you for any alienating behavior you've engaged in. Ask Him to help you forgive your ex for whatever they've done to you. We are often so willing to acknowledge God's infinite forgiveness with one exception: our ex. Our pain, fear, and bitterness try to convince us that our ex is the *one person in the world* who doesn't deserve forgiveness, either from God or from us. But that's just not true—God's forgiveness is for us *all*.

Third, go the extra mile by actively inserting positive thoughts and actions and by exercising the fruit of the Spirit in your heart regarding your ex. The best way to turn the tide on years of pain and bitterness is to start praying for the person. Ask God to bless them and their new family. Ask God to enrich your child's relationship with their other parent and stepfamily, giving the child a healthy and happy experience with both parents. That doesn't just help create a healing environment for your child; it also helps you uproot any bitterness that's negatively affecting your life. Prayer will change you, and it will change your circumstances.

You cannot *hate* someone your child *loves*—especially if that person is their other parent. Whether you make a big, dramatic show of your feelings or do your best to keep them to yourself, your child will notice them. Even if you are known for holding your tongue, your child will infer from your eye rolls, facial expressions, body language, huffs, and grumbles that you hate their other parent, and the enemy will use that to ultimately drive a wedge between you.

A parent's attempts to "punish" or "get back at" their ex become a poison in their relationship with their child, slowly and quietly polluting the relationship until the kid can't stand to be around *either* parent. Even if you "win" the battle against your ex (though in these cases, no one is a true winner), you could lose your relationship with the child. Those stakes are too high and costly to risk.

The better option, though we know it often feels impossible, is to follow Jesus' call: "Love your enemies, do good to those who hate you, bless those who curse you, pray for those who abuse you" (Luke 6:27–28). Remember, the real enemy is Satan, not your ex. By loving those who hate you, you are doing exactly what the enemy doesn't want you to do.

Sometimes we express resentment subtly. We may not say anything, but everything else about our behavior makes it clear what we think about our ex. Other times, we are loud and proud with our resentment, putting it on full display for all to see. We want *everyone*, including our child, to know what we think of our ex.

Why do otherwise mature, full-grown adults act like this? We're sure there are many reasons, but one seems to come up most often: it's a power play. They want to make themselves look bigger, better, and more loving in the eyes of the child by making the other parent look smaller, worse, and resentful. Over time, we can get stuck in a negative behavior cycle that isn't just sad; it's also counterproductive to what we should be working toward. It's actually taking us further away from the thing we want most—a close relationship with the child. Children want to take both parents to the summit. They'll gladly go with one, but they'd rather have both. And God wants them to have both.

As parents wanting the very best for our kids, we've got to be mindful of how we're using our influence in an honoring, Kingdom-minded way. When we're constantly belittling the other parent in front of the child, we're using our parental influence in a negative way, hoping to bring disruption and disunity into the child's relationship with the other parent. God is a God of peace and unity, not resentment and division. Scripture calls all children to *honor* their mother and father. Why would we want to turn their godly love for their mother or father into ungodly hate?

When we lift up the other parent and celebrate their relationship with the child, we're using our parental influence in a positive way that enriches the child's relationship with both parents. We're showing our children the power of God in our own lives—the power to transform the resentment we feel into love and to bring grace where there was condemnation.

To have a connection with other people—especially people we don't particularly like—we must learn to love them in Christ and see them through His eyes. If we don't, then we create an environment of disconnection and disunity, and that's exactly what the enemy wants. We cannot let the devil steal the institution of family! The best weapon we have to fight back against his schemes is a loving, grace-filled attitude toward the person with whom we're raising a child. The enemy has already broken up one home; don't let him break up any more.

RECOMMENDED SCRIPTURE READING

See to it that no one fails to obtain the grace of God; that no "root of bitterness" springs up and causes trouble (Hebrews 12:15).

Above all else, guard your heart, for everything you do flows from it (Proverbs 4:23 NIV).

God gave us a spirit not of fear but of power and love and self-control (2 Timothy 1:7).

For you did not receive the spirit of slavery to fall back into fear, but you have received the Spirit of adoption as sons, by whom we cry, "Abba! Father!" (Romans 8:15).

The thief comes *only* to steal and kill and destroy (John 10:10, emphasis added).

Love your enemies, do good to those who hate you, bless those who curse you, pray for those who abuse you (Luke 6:27–28).

DISCUSSION QUESTIONS

1. Why does your attitude about your ex-spouse have a huge impact on your children?

_____

_____

_____

_____

2. What steps can parents take to avoid subconsciously manipulating or alienating their children?

_____

_____

_____

_____

3. What do you think would happen if parents stopped giving into fear and started taking authority over the enemy?

4. How does forgiveness open the door for God's blessings on a family?

REFLECTION QUESTIONS

1. What are two ways you can help your children feel "at home" at both houses?

2. How have your words and actions affected your children's relationship with their other biological parent?

3. What does the enemy want for your family? What does God want for your family?

_____

_____

_____

_____

PRAYER

Father God, we want to model the character of Your Son, Jesus, in all our relationships. Please teach us to guard our hearts and minds against all unforgiveness or resentment toward our ex-spouse. We release all bitterness towards them, and we ask You to bless them. Give us wisdom as we model Your grace and kindness for our children. May they feel Your peace in our home and in their spirits. In Jesus' name, Amen.

ASSIGNMENT
- Read Chapter 9 in *Blended and Redeemed*.
- Ask the Lord, "What do You want to teach me?"

CHAPTER 9

LITIGATION: YOUR NEW, LEAST-FAVORITE HOBBY

"The best goal for litigation is a resolution you can live with and that is good for the child."

▬ ICEBREAKER

What is your favorite hobby or pastime?

▬ RECAP

You are a part of *one* blended family, but your child is a part of *two*. Making your child more comfortable in their back-and-forth way of life is something that's easily fixed with attention to accommodations and communication. Wherever the child is, they never stop having two parents, and making the child feel at home and well-connected to both parents is your responsibility.

Child manipulation is the way a parent tries to control a child's thoughts or feelings. Parent alienation is the act of manipulating a child to dislike or cut off the other parent relationship. Fear, rejection, and shame create a heavy emotional burden that is not from God, and we must learn to guard our words and actions in order to avoid transferring bitterness and resentment to our children.

You cannot *hate* someone your child *loves*—especially if that person is their other parent. When we lift up the other parent and celebrate their relationship with the child, we're using our parental influence in a positive way that enriches the child's relationship with *both* parents.

▃ REVIEW

The litigation journey can have several different entry points, much like a highway has several different onramps. There are different processes for litigation as well, meaning different ways to get to a resolution, but there are primarily two reasons why one or both parents may begin a formal litigation process to revise the custody arrangement outlined in their initial divorce/custody papers:

1. If something has changed.
2. If the child's safety is at risk.

What do we mean by "something has changed"? It could mean anything from a remarriage to a move to a change in finances. It can be terrifying to crack open the papers and put yourselves and your children back into the legal system. But if the original agreement isn't working out for whatever reason, it's time to take a fresh look at things.

This doesn't mean, however, that your first step is to hire a lawyer and draw up an attack plan. In fact, we think this should be the last step to take and only if you have to. There are a few less dramatic, less disruptive steps to take before then. The exception is if the child's safety is at risk, a situation in which you should take immediate action.

The goal—the best outcome—of litigation, whether through mediation or a full-blown court case, is a resolution you can live with and that is good for the child. Almost no one walks out of family court or mediation feeling like they got everything they wanted, but it's not about getting everything you want—it's about getting something you can live with. This usually requires the grownups to choke down their pride and frustration and make a sacrifice in the best interests of the child, whether that's a sacrifice of time, money, convenience, or opportunity.

Being in a lawsuit is a lot like driving down the highway. Everything is going by so fast. Every mile or two, you come to an exit, but most of them are blocked and inaccessible. Even if you want to take them, you can't. But whenever you find an exit you *can* take that gets you off the highway of litigation, *you should take it*. It won't take you exactly where you wanted to go or lead you to everything you hoped for, but if it gets you somewhere safe, take it. You may not have a better option—or any other option whatsoever—further down the road.

Going back to court with your ex takes a lot of time and causes emotional and mental anguish for everyone involved (especially the children). The outcome is almost never what you think it is going to be. Litigation should never be taken lightly. Before jumping into a lawsuit with your ex, exhaust all other options. Litigation should be the *last* resort. Once a lawsuit begins and a judge gets involved, everything gets more difficult, painful, stressful, and expensive at every level. Litigation can bring out the worst in people, and the whole ordeal is painful, heartbreaking, and embarrassing. It can seem nearly impossible to go through that and maintain any kind of healthy, positive relationship with your ex.

We should do our best to stay out of court because that's what God has called us to do (see Matthew 18:15–20). We want the legal system to be our very last option. If we can try to work out a resolution with the other person in peace, unity, and respect, just like Scripture tells us, we should always do that.

Litigation is spiritual warfare. The real enemy in our custody conflicts isn't our ex—it's the devil. He hates our families, and he will do anything he can to tear them apart and destroy our children's futures. By striking at our family stability, the enemy seeks to disrupt our overall sense of peace and satisfaction in life. But God has not left us unarmed and unprepared for our spiritual conflicts. He gives us six pieces of spiritual armor (see Ephesians 6:13–18), strengthened and held together by the power of prayer, that can and will equip us for the legal battle ahead.

Litigation is really expensive. If you're going to make it through your litigation process, you've got to have a realistic understanding of your budget from the outset. Lawsuits usually begin at a very emotional level, which leads people to make horrible financial decisions that they may not even realize until they're further down the road. Before you ever set foot inside a courtroom, you've got to pay for attorney retainers, depositions, interviews, discovery research, and investigation—and that's just to get to court. You could spend a year or more preparing for the actual trial. If you aren't careful, you'll run out of money long before you ever see a judge.

Be sure to make decisions when you are calm and feel peace from the Holy Spirit to do so. Take a breath, step back, spend time in prayer, and make an honest evaluation of your heart, your thoughts, and how much money you can reasonably afford to spend on this. We know that fighting for your parental rights and for the safety of your child shouldn't be all about money—and it's not—but the harsh reality is that money is a big part of it. This will become a huge financial burden for your family, so go into it with your eyes open.

Guard your expectations. There are no real "winners" in any litigation, regardless of what the judge decides. Too often, someone is motivated by wanting the other party to lose just as much as they are by wanting themselves to win. The reality is that both parties will win *and* lose. Take advantage of compromises that could end things quickly, especially if those compromises are ultimately what's best for the child. Refusing to do so could ruin your marriage, your finances, and your relationship with your children.

The family court system has developed a fairly robust process for avoiding full-blown litigation. There are options that enable you to work together with your ex in a less stressful situation to come up with new agreements and decree revisions that are just as legally binding as a court order but don't come with a year's worth of discovery, depositions, and courtroom shenanigans.

First, work with your ex toward a solution. If you have a reasonably good relationship with your ex-spouse and the need arises to change the custody arrangement, your first step should be to sit down together and have a civil conversation. If you have a contentious relationship with your ex, this approach may sound like a fantasy, but we've seen God work miracles in these conversations when no one would have expected it. A prolonged legal battle is almost never what is best for the child, so do anything you can to avoid it—even if this means inviting your ex over for lunch to hash things out one on one.

Second, engage a parent facilitator. Generally, a parent facilitator is named in your divorce papers as a resource to help you avoid unnecessary legal action as you work together to raise your child. This can be a fantastic resource for ex-spouses who just needed a little nudge and an unbiased third party to work with to reach relatively simple decisions. Parent facilitators help cut through the noise and get you to a solution faster and easier.

Third, work through a mediator. Once you get into mediation, the assumption is that neither party can come to an agreement. Mediation is a good solution when one party wants to make more significant changes to their custody arrangement that would otherwise require the court's active involvement. Parents agree to work through a mediator to find the best, most appropriate, and most child-focused solution.

If you've gone through the previous steps and are still unable to resolve your disagreement, or if your ex is unwilling to work with you using any of the methods mentioned above, then you might find yourself in the unfortunate situation of a lawsuit. You will need a good lawyer, one who is led by the Holy Spirit and good at family law. They understand your unique situation, give practical advice you can act on, have experience with cases similar to your own, and understand and respect your budget. Interview several attorneys to find the one who is the best fit for you. This is someone who will spend months fighting your most important, personal battle, so don't rush into a decision. Take the time to get to know your options and ultimately find someone you can trust to handle your case on your behalf.

Here are five tips for choosing the right attorney:

1. Choose someone local.
2. Set clear expectations.
3. Check for relevant experience.
4. Stick with the same attorney for the long haul.
5. Pick an attorney you have a personal connection with.

You want a man or woman of God who is going to act with integrity and cover your case with prayer, seeking God's wisdom for every decision throughout the entire ordeal. In our experience, the best attorney is the one who can integrate their professional experience with biblical principles (confirmed through Scripture) and draw their knowledge and decision-making from this.

As we said before, litigation is spiritual warfare. It is a shockingly chaotic situation, and the enemy *loves* chaos. But he should have no place in our custody decisions! Strive to fill your legal army with as many believers as you can, "for the LORD is our judge; the LORD is our lawgiver; the LORD is our king; he will save us" (Isaiah 33:22).

Whether you're the one serving the papers or the one receiving the papers, we recommend keeping these five warnings in mind throughout the process:

1. Don't jump right into action.

   Emotions run hot and high during a lawsuit—especially when your child is involved. There will be plenty of time for action but not the first day or two. Spend time in prayer seeking God's peace and direction and preparing your heart for the spiritual battle ahead.

2. Don't engage in social media.

   It's wise to get off social media completely during this season. You never, ever want to air your lawsuit business in any public forum, whether it's social media or the break room at work. Anything you say, especially anything you *write* and publish for the world to see, will come back to bite you in court.

3. **Don't try to go it alone.**
   Litigation will be a long, trying process. Surround yourself with people who love you, who will commit to pray for you, and who can offer wise counsel. Above all, surround yourself with people you can *trust*. However, resist the urge to talk about the litigation in detail because anyone you talk to could be called as a witness.
4. **Don't unburden yourself to your child.**
   Do not share your frustrations in detail with your child. This puts an undue burden on the child and causes them to feel like they must pick one parent over the other. They have enough to deal with just trying to figure out how *they* feel about everything that's going on; they don't need to try to deal with *your* feelings too.
5. **Don't let fear steal your parental authority.**
   When everything you say and do is scrutinized under a microscope, you may feel like you could lose your child if you do or say anything wrong. Intense pressure can make you say, do, think, and act in ways that are not reasonable or realistic. Ask God for revelation, tell the enemy that he has no place in your home, and reclaim your power!

Having to go through a lengthy court battle is rarely what's best, but neither is losing a parent to fear. So be bold. Be brave. Take care of all the legal things that demand your attention, but never stop parenting your child. After all, that is what you're fighting this whole battle for!

RECOMMEND SCRIPTURE READING

For the Lord is our judge; the Lord is our lawgiver;
the Lord is our king; he will save us (Isaiah 33:22).

If your brother sins against you, go and tell him his fault, between you and him alone. If he listens to you, you have gained your brother. But if he does not listen, take one or two others along with you, that every charge may be established by the evidence of two or three witnesses. If he refuses to listen to them, tell it to the church. And if he refuses to listen even to the church, let him be to you as a Gentile and a tax collector (Matthew 18:15–17).

For we do not wrestle against flesh and blood, but against the rulers, against the authorities, against the cosmic powers over this present darkness, against the spiritual forces of evil in the heavenly places. Therefore take up the whole armor of God, that you may be able to withstand in the evil day, and having done all, to stand firm. Stand therefore, having fastened on the belt of truth, and having put on the breastplate of righteousness, and, as shoes for your feet, having put on the readiness given by the gospel of peace. In all circumstances take up the shield of faith, with which you can extinguish all the flaming darts of the evil one; and take the helmet of salvation, and the sword of the Spirit, which is the word of God, praying at all times in the Spirit, with all prayer and supplication (Ephesians 6:12–18).

Therefore do not be anxious, saying, "What shall we eat?" or "What shall we drink?" or "What shall we wear?" For the Gentiles seek after all these things, and your heavenly Father knows that you need them all. But seek *first* the kingdom of God and his righteousness, and all these things will be added to you (Matthew 6:31–33, emphasis added).

DISCUSSION QUESTIONS

1. Why does litigation tend to bring out the worst in people?

2. Why are there no real "winners" in any litigation?

3. What are the most important characteristics of a godly lawyer?

4. How should believers respond when litigation becomes difficult, confusing, or unfair?

REFLECTION QUESTIONS

1. What legal measures have you tried before going through litigation? What measures would you like to try?

2. How can you protect your child's mind and heart during the litigation process?

3. Have you given up any power to the enemy through fear or discouragement? What do you need to do to take it back?

PRAYER

Father God, thank You for being with us in the best and worst moments of our lives. We trust that no matter what happens, You will never leave us. We take authority over the enemy who wants to destroy our families, and we declare that all power belongs to the Lord Jesus. We will not give into fear. We will stand firm in our faith that with You, all things are possible, and we trust You for the future of our family. In Jesus' name, Amen.

ASSIGNMENT

- Read Chapter 10 in *Blended and Redeemed*.
- Ask the Lord, "What do You want to teach me?"

CHAPTER 10

BLENDED FAMILIES, GOD'S REDEMPTION

"Our families are a collection—a reflection—of our broken pieces, masterfully rearranged by God into a beautiful mosaic."

ICEBREAKER

What is your favorite story of redemption in the Bible?

RECAP

The goal for litigation is a resolution you can live with and that is good for the child. Going back to court with your ex takes a lot of time and causes emotional and mental anguish for everyone involved (especially the children). Before jumping into a lawsuit, exhaust all other options, such as working with your ex, engaging a parent facilitator, and working through a mediator. Recognize that litigation is spiritual warfare. The real enemy is the devil, not your ex. Litigation is also really expensive, and there are no real "winners," regardless of the judge's decision.

If a lawsuit is unavoidable, find a local, experienced lawyer who is led by the Holy Spirit, respectful of your budget, and understanding of your expectations. Don't jump right into action; spend time in prayer seeking God's peace and direction and preparing your heart for the spiritual battle ahead. Don't engage in social media, because anything you say, write, or post can hurt you in court. Don't try to go it alone, though; surround yourself with people you can trust. Don't unburden yourself to your child, because they have enough to deal with as they try to figure out their own feelings. Finally, don't let fear steal your parental authority. Take care of all the legal things that demand your attention, but never stop parenting your child.

REVIEW

Redemption is a major theme throughout the Bible. Story after story shows us how God worked miracles in the lives of everyday men and women—people just like us—to save them from slavery, famine, sickness, oppression, and ultimately, their own sin. It was true for Noah, Moses, Ruth, King David, Nicodemus, Zacchaeus, Matthew the tax collector, and Paul. It is true for us (Scott and Vanessa), and it is true for you and your family.

Our God is a redeeming God, and He loves to redeem our lives from the mess and madness we often find ourselves stuck in. Nowhere is that more evident than in the life of a blended family. From day one, a blended family comes pre-loaded with some of the most painful and potentially explosive baggage imaginable, even under the best of circumstances. There are new spouses, new siblings, new homes, new schools, and new routines slamming up against old wounds, old mistrust, old relationships, and old lives. It's a lot, and sometimes, like Ruth, we can start to feel completely lost and alone.

But we're not lost and alone. We have a Redeemer working *with* us and fighting *for* us. We are building our new families on the firm foundation of Jesus Christ. We are placing our trust in a God of redemption, healing, and forgiveness. He wants to bless you and your family, and He *is* blessing you and your family, even when life seems harder than you can bear.

The mission verse for our Blended Kingdom Families ministry is Luke 1:37: "For nothing will be impossible with God." God gave us that verse at the outset of the ministry because He knew this blended family life would often *seem* impossible. Most blended families we know have already walked through the fire or are in the midst of it. But here's the good news: *God is fireproof*. He'll walk with you through the most intense heat and deliver you safely out the other side.

When we're making Kingdom-based decisions, we're looking for every opportunity to draw closer to God, especially when we're in the fire. Sometimes, we carry God into the fire with us. Other times, we find Him there waiting for us. Whatever your relationship is with Him now and whatever your experience has been with Him in past, we want to encourage you to run to God in the fire. He is there, and He is waiting for you. He is your place of peace, a shelter and refuge. He is the one who can not only protect you from the flames but can also refine you—*redeem* you—through the process. Because Christ has redeemed us, we can claim the abundant life He promised us (see John 10:10). We can live a *Kingdom* life.

We see in the book of Daniel that God walked Shadrach, Meshach, and Abednego through the fire and delivered them safely out of the furnace. What happened as a result? God Himself received the glory! Nebuchadnezzar finally knew whom he was dealing with and decreed that God's name would be honored throughout the land: "For there is no other god who is able to rescue in this way" (Daniel 3:29).

Of course, having faith as our foundation does not prevent us from going through the fire any more than it protected Shadrach, Meshach, and Abednego from being tossed in the furnace. In fact, like them, choosing to live by godly principles might be the thing that causes us to go through the fire. Jesus even told us to expect this: "In this world *you will have trouble*. But take heart! I have overcome the world" (John 16:33 NIV, emphasis added). Yes, it's hard to believe this is promised to us, but the spiritual reality is that miracles happen in the fire. When we come through it, we emerge with a pure heart, authority, developed faith, scars of hope, and a testimony that not only helps other families but also builds the faith of our children.

Despite God's promise of redemption, you'll often hear the term "broken home." We don't like that term. Your home isn't broken if it's built on the foundation of Jesus Christ. That's the only firm foundation that can weather the storms of life. Even in the mess and ruins of the destruction, God still has you in His capable hands. He is still there holding you up. The foundation is still secure, and only God knows what might be rebuilt on that foundation.

Brokenness is part of all our stories, but we are not defined by brokenness. In fact, there can be beauty in brokenness. Brokenness is something we *go through*; it is not *who we are*. That's why it's misguided to say that you are a broken home. No, brokenness is something that your family has been through. It is an event, not a condition. It is something that happens, not a state of being.

Who you are—your state of being—is defined by Christ. We have an identity in Christ. He (and only He) tells us who we are, and He says we are chosen, loved, and set apart (Colossians 3:12). We are fearfully and wonderfully made (Psalm 139:14). We are heirs to the Kingdom and co-heirs with Him (Romans 8:17). We are children of the Most High God (Galatians 3:26–29). Our families are a collection—a reflection—of our broken pieces, masterfully rearranged by God into a beautiful mosaic. And like a mosaic, the beauty is not *in spite of* our brokenness but *because of* our brokenness.

Nothing makes us feel more broken and alone than the breakup of a family unit and the terrifying prospect of your child losing the stability of "home" with Mom and Dad. These life events are tragedies. They are understandably sources of pain, guilt, shame, regret, and grief. But God offers hope in our grief. We are not left to make sense of the madness alone.

> The lifeblood of our ministry is wrapped up in Isaiah 61:1–3:
> He has sent me to bind up the brokenhearted
> To proclaim freedom for the captives
> And release from darkness for the prisoners ...
> to comfort all who mourn,
> and provide for those who grieve in Zion—

to bestow on them a crown of beauty
instead of ashes,
the oil of joy
instead of mourning,
and a garment of praise
instead of a spirit of despair (NIV, emphasis added).

This is the word of hope we share with families who are struggling to make sense of their blended-family situation. We read it as a promise from God, who wants to exchange our captivity for freedom, our filthy ashes for a beautiful crown, our mourning for joy, and our rags for splendor. In the same way, we know He wants to take any concept of a "broken home" and exchange it for a happy, healthy, and loving home filled with joy and praise.

When you're standing there in the dust of a relationship or family unit that's just crumbled away, it's easy to feel hopeless. We feel anything *but* royal. That's when God steps in, picks us up out of the dirt and dust, cleans us off, and reminds us that we are sons and daughters of the Most High God! Not only does God give us a crown, but He also anoints us with "the oil of joy," a common biblical practice most often associated with times of celebration, not sorrow. He removes the dirty, stained clothes of our "spirit of despair" and covers us with the "garment of praise." The language here points to clothes dyed in bright colors. God is dressing us for a party, not a funeral! He's preparing us for life, not death! And why does God do this? The end of Isaiah 61:3 answers: "They will be called oaks of righteousness ... for the display of *his* splendor" (emphasis added).

This is exactly what happened when Shadrach, Meshach, and Abednego emerged from the fiery furnace unscathed. The king and all who were there were astounded by the power of the God who saved them. What a stunning reminder that God can and will redeem our worst circumstances—even the breakup of a family—in miraculous ways. And when God does what only He can do, everyone wins—us, our children, the community, and ultimately God Himself!

A year after I (Vanessa) had the experience I discussed in chapter 1, life had returned to normal, and our litigation had come to a (miraculous) conclusion. Our family was on much firmer footing, and God visited me once again in my dreams. I stood in a barren field, and in each hand, I held an old tree stump that was pulsing with electricity. When I threw the stumps to the ground, new roots shot deep into the soil, and the stumps grew into tall, wide, and mighty oak trees reaching for the heavens. Behind those two trees, I saw four other trees spring up, creating four neat rows, and those trees grew just as deep, tall, and wide as the first two. As I pondered these things, I heard a voice say, "This is your legacy orchard."

New trees continued to spring up, row after row, with a clear path that started between the first two trees. I knew that path led to the Father. Suddenly, a rope fell from heaven between the first two trees, which I understood represented Scott and me. I began climbing the rope, and the higher I got, the more trees I could see in the distance. I climbed a few more feet and looked out over the trees, and I saw a massive orchard of the most amazing trees, full of perfect fruit, lined up in endless rows going all the way to the Father. I was looking at generations of our family, starting with Scott and me, then to our four sons, and then out into the far, far future.

Suddenly, I found myself on the other end of the orchard. I was standing on the path that started with the first two trees, but I was different. I was a little girl. Jesus stood next to me, and I felt an overwhelming sense of joy. So I danced. There I was, this perfectly happy and content little girl, dancing next to Jesus as the angels clapped along.

The memory of this dream has changed the way I read Isaiah 61:3. In His amazing grace, God showed me a glimpse of the "oaks of righteousness" He was raising up in the Martindale family. That's how I know this legacy is a critical part of His plan for us, for His church, and for all families, blended or not. He is doing an important work, and He's doing it through our families—because that's the only way each of us can extend our values, priorities, and faith into the far, far future.

What we love about our blended family—and what, hopefully, you love about yours—is that God took what the enemy meant for evil and turned it into good. He took the ashes and turned them into a crown. And through that process, we became grounded and firm in our foundation with Christ. He planted our roots deep into that foundation of faith, and He's held us tightly ever since. Just knowing that blended families can be blessed—that your second, third, or fourth marriage can *truly* be blessed—and that you are an heir to the Kingdom of God ... well, it's incredible.

The breakdown of society begins with the breakdown of the family unit. If the enemy can get to our children, he can destroy our legacies. If he destroys our legacies, then he controls the world. Kingdom legacy is all about breaking generational curses. It's about teaching and training our children in the Word. It's about showing our children what godly, healthy marriages look like. It's loving others as Christ loves us. It's living a life of forgiveness. It's embracing restoration. It's accepting our position as a new creation in Christ. It's remembering that we are who we are *right now*, not who we were *back then*. Legacy is, in effect, a generational game-changer.

Our legacy as individuals, as spouses, and as parents depends on our relationship with Jesus. Can you be a good husband, wife, mom, or dad and not be a Christian? Sure. But will that impact be enough to fight back the schemes of the enemy over several generations of your family tree? Whether we make it to 30 or 130, we have precious little time on this earth to make a real impact on the world and on the generations to come. What we pour into our children makes a big difference, but we're still so very limited in what we're able to accomplish with our human hands.

God has no limits. He's infinite. When we partner Him in our marriage, in rearing our kids, in serving other people, or in anything else, we are tapping into that endless, amazing, eternal life and power that will carry on generation after generation. When you introduce your children to that infinite power, you extend your legacy even further.

To build a home on the firm foundation of Jesus Christ, you first need to have a relationship with Him. Jesus Himself stated plainly, "For God so loved the world, that he gave his only Son, that whoever believes in him should not perish but have eternal life" (John 3:16). It's Christ and Christ alone who puts the *Kingdom* in your blended Kingdom family!

RECOMMENDED SCRIPTURE READING

He has sent me to bind up the brokenhearted
To proclaim freedom for the captives
And release from darkness for the prisoners ...
to comfort all who mourn,
and provide for those who grieve in Zion—
to bestow on them a crown of beauty
instead of ashes,
the oil of joy
instead of mourning,
and a garment of praise
instead of a spirit of despair (Isaiah 61:1-3 NIV, emphasis added).

For there is no other god who is able to rescue in this way (Daniel 3:29).

In this world *you will have trouble*. But take heart! I have overcome the world (John 16:33 NIV, emphasis added).

Now to him who is able to do far more abundantly than all that we ask or think, according to the power at work within us, to him be glory in the church and in Christ Jesus throughout all generations, forever and ever. Amen (Ephesians 3:20–21).

Everyone who calls on the name of the Lord will be saved (Romans 10:13).

For the wages of sin is death, but the free gift of God is eternal life in Christ Jesus our Lord (Romans 6:23).

DISCUSSION QUESTIONS

1. How can we live a Kingdom life even while we are walking through fire?

   _____

   _____

   _____

   _____

2. Instead of "broken homes," what are positive ways to describe blended families?

   _____

   _____

   _____

   _____

3. According to Scripture, what is our identity in Christ?

   _____

   _____

   _____

   _____

4. Why does the enemy target the family unit? How can we protect our children?

▰ REFLECTION QUESTIONS

1. In what ways have you already seen God's redemption in your family?

2. Read Luke 1:37. What "impossible" things are you still trusting God to do?

3. How can you begin to establish a Kingdom legacy for your family?

PRAYER

Father God, You are a God of redemption. You have been faithful to walk with us through the fires of life, and You will continue to be faithful as You replace our ashes with crowns of beauty. Thank You for rearranging the pieces of our broken lives into a new work of art. We choose today to establish our families on the firm foundation of Jesus Christ. We receive Him as our Lord and Savior, and we commit to building a Kingdom legacy. In Jesus' name, Amen.

ASSIGNMENT
- Ask the Lord, "What do You want to teach me?"
- Celebrate!

APPENDIX

SALVATION

What is the most important relationship in your life? Some people might think of their spouse, their children, or their best friend. These are certainly special people who impact your life, but there is another relationship that is even more important, because this Person impacts your eternity. This Person is God. Do you have a relationship with Him?

God created humans in His image. Why? Because He loves us and wants to have a relationship with us! God is a loving Father, and He desires to have every person on earth as part of His family. There's just one problem—sin. That's the Bible's term for everything wrong we say or do. You see, God is perfect and holy, so sin cannot exist in His presence. This creates quite the dilemma for us because the Bible says, "All have sinned and fall short of the glory of God" (Romans 3:23). There is no such thing as a perfect person. We all sin, and sin separates us from God. There is nothing we can do to fix this problem; we cannot buy, earn, beg, or cheat our way into heaven.

Thankfully, there is a Divine Solution: Jesus Christ. John 3:16, the most famous verse in the Bible, says, "For God so loved the world, that he gave his only Son, that whoever believes in him should not perish but have eternal life." Jesus surrendered Himself as the perfect sacrifice, saving us from separation from God and offering us eternal life with Him. What an amazing Savior!

God will never force you to accept His offer of forgiveness. He gives every person the gift of free will, which means you can choose to accept or reject His salvation. If you choose to reject His salvation, you will have to struggle through life with your own strength and be separated from the Lord. However, if you accept God's salvation, you will never be alone for a single moment for the rest of eternity. God will give you His Holy Spirit to be your Teacher, Comforter, and Guide, and you will have the power to live a godly life. Every part of your existence will be affected—for the better! Salvation doesn't mean you will become a perfect person, but it does mean that you will do life with the only Person who is perfect, and He changes *everything*.

Would you like to begin your relationship with God today? It's not complicated or difficult. Romans 10:9 says, "If you confess with your mouth that Jesus is Lord and believe in your heart that God raised him from the dead, you will be saved." If your answer is yes, then pray this prayer out loud or in your heart. Feel free to add your own words if you would like.

Father God, I admit that I am a sinner in need of Your loving grace. I repent of my sins and confess with my mouth that Jesus Christ is Your Son who died on the cross to pay the price for my sins. I believe that You raised Him from the dead. I ask You, Jesus, to come into my heart, and I believe by faith that You are now my Lord and Savior. I receive Your Holy Spirit to guide and to help me do Your will. I believe and receive Your eternal gift of life that I have prayed for today. In Jesus' name, Amen.

If you prayed this prayer and truly meant it, then please allow us to welcome you into the family of God! We are so excited to count you as our brother or sister in Christ. Your old life has stopped, and your new life has begun. We encourage you to share this wonderful news with your spouse and children.

WATER BAPTISM

Before He returned to heaven to be with His Father, Jesus gave His disciples these instructions:

> Go therefore and make disciples of all nations, baptizing them in the name of the Father and of the Son and of the Holy Spirit (Matthew 28:19).

The baptism Jesus is referring to in this verse is water baptism—a person's total immersion in water. Why is water baptism important? It is the first act of obedience God requires of believers, and it is a physical representation of the death, burial, and resurrection of Jesus. Romans 6:4 says, "We were buried therefore with him by **baptism** into death, in order that, just as Christ was raised from the dead by the glory of the Father, we too might walk in newness of life" (emphasis added). Think of it this way: when you go into the water, you put to death your past life of sin. It is buried and gone for all eternity. Then, when you rise out of the water, you are raised to a brand-new life in Jesus. No longer held down by the weight of guilt or shame, you are free to live in the power and blessing of the Holy Spirit.

You may have been previously baptized as young child or even as an adult, but the Bible teaches that water baptism should occur *after* a person has received salvation. Please don't feel embarrassed if you need to be water baptized again. It is a wonderful opportunity to proclaim to the world that you surrendered your life to the lordship of Jesus. Pastor Jimmy Evans explains it this way:

> Water baptism is the seal of the covenant between Christ and believers. It is our first public step of obedience and shows our good faith in making Jesus the Lord of our lives. Without being water baptized you will never have the same level of confidence about your standing with the Lord, and

you won't experience the supernatural miracle that happens in your heart through baptism.[2]

Ask a pastor or a Christian friend or family member to baptize you as soon as possible. It doesn't matter if it occurs in a church baptistry, a lake, a swimming pool, or any other body of water. You will be so grateful that you obeyed the Lord and took this incredible step of obedience.

---

[2] Jimmy Evans, *Tipping Point* (Dallas, Texas: XO Publishing, 2020), 236.

FINDING A CHURCH

> I was glad when they said to me, "Let us go to the house of the Lord!" —Psalm 122:1

God did not design you to live the Christian life alone. You need support from people who love the Lord and will encourage you in your walk with Christ. The writer of Hebrews instructs us,

> Let us consider how to stir up one another to love and good works, **not neglecting to meet together, as is the habit of some, but encouraging one another**, and all the more as you see the Day drawing near (10:24–25, emphasis added).

There is no better place to surround yourself with fellow believers than the local church. When trying to find a healthy, Bible-believing church, you may come across a wide variety of service types, programs, and activities. It is important to find the best fit for your family, and it may take several attempts to find the right place.

The most important question to ask yourself when considering a church to call "home" is this: **Does this church teach what the Bible says?** In today's world, it's sadly more and more common for pastors and teachers to stray from using the Bible as their foundation for truth. Ask to see the church's statement of faith and find out what their position is on crucial biblical issues, such as salvation, water baptism, the divinity of Christ, and the authority of Scripture. The right church will be rooted firmly in Scripture and will be able provide a scripturally accurate basis for its teachings.

Finding the right church will change your life! Your family will be strengthened as you grow together in the Lord, and you will be forever blessed by the relationships you build with your brothers and sisters in Christ.

ABOUT THE AUTHORS

Blended family experts Scott and Vanessa Martindale have been where you are. Living blended their entire lives, they know firsthand both the joys and difficulties that can come along with it.

The Martindales founded Blended Kingdom Families (BKF) in 2020 with a passionate desire to equip and encourage blended families and married couples and to help the local church cultivate community among blended families. Scott and Vanessa believe blended families have suffered far too long in silence, and now is their time for restoration and redemption. Through faith and radical obedience, Scott and Vanessa have partnered with God to better equip the local church to reach blended families. BKF exists to break the generational cycle of divorce by equipping marriages and uniting blended families with the truth of God's Word.

Scott is a Licensed Professional Counselor, and for more than 15 years he has helped couples, marriages, and families on their journey through life's challenges. Vanessa is a registered nurse, and she is pursuing a master's degree in Marriage and Family Therapy at The King's University. Scott and Vanessa reside in the Dallas-Fort Worth Metroplex with their sons Michael, Shay, Gray, and Kace.

XO MARRIAGE RESOURCES

21 Day Inner Healing Journey
A step-by-step guide to emotional health that guides you from toxic thoughts, emotional wounds, and bondages from your past into total inner healing. Through 21 daily lessons and personal application exercises, this incredible book helps you transform your life and relationships.

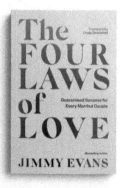

The Four Laws of Love
Jimmy Evans outlines the foundational pillars upon which God designed marriage. Without holding back, he tells the story of his own marriages, which was hurtling toward divorce until this self-proclaimed "bad husband" came to recognize and put into practice these four laws.

Vision Retreat Guidebook
In this powerful guidebook, couples take a journey into the areas of spiritual and personal growth, preparation, and vision for their family. Serving as a hands-on practical tool, the information contained in this journal leads couples to address important topics such as marriage priorities and values. With thought-provoking questions, couples can record milestone events, family accomplishments, and much more while creating a family keepsake to reference for years to come.

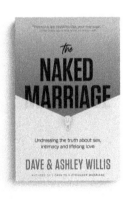

The Naked Marriage
Having a "Naked Marriage" is much more than just nakedness in the bedroom. It means being naked emotionally and spiritually as well as physically. It also means undressing all the misconceptions our culture has used to cover God's original, beautiful design for marriage and rediscovering all marriage can be.

store.xomarriage.com